Alison O'Brien lives in Belfast where she works as a journalist with the *Irish News*. This is her first book.

Paddy Joseph Grimshaw was born in Belfast in 1944. He has spent most of his adult life trying to find his mother and discover why she abandoned him. Paddy lives in a residential home in Ballyclare, County Down.

ABANDONED

ABANDONED

A Survivor's Story

ALISON O'BRIEN

THE BREHON PRESS
BELFAST

First published 2008 by
The Brehon Press Ltd
1A Bryson Street,
Belfast BT5 4ES,
Northern Ireland

ISBN: 978 1 905474 25 7

Cover design: December Publications
Printed and bound by JH Haynes & Co Ltd, Sparkford

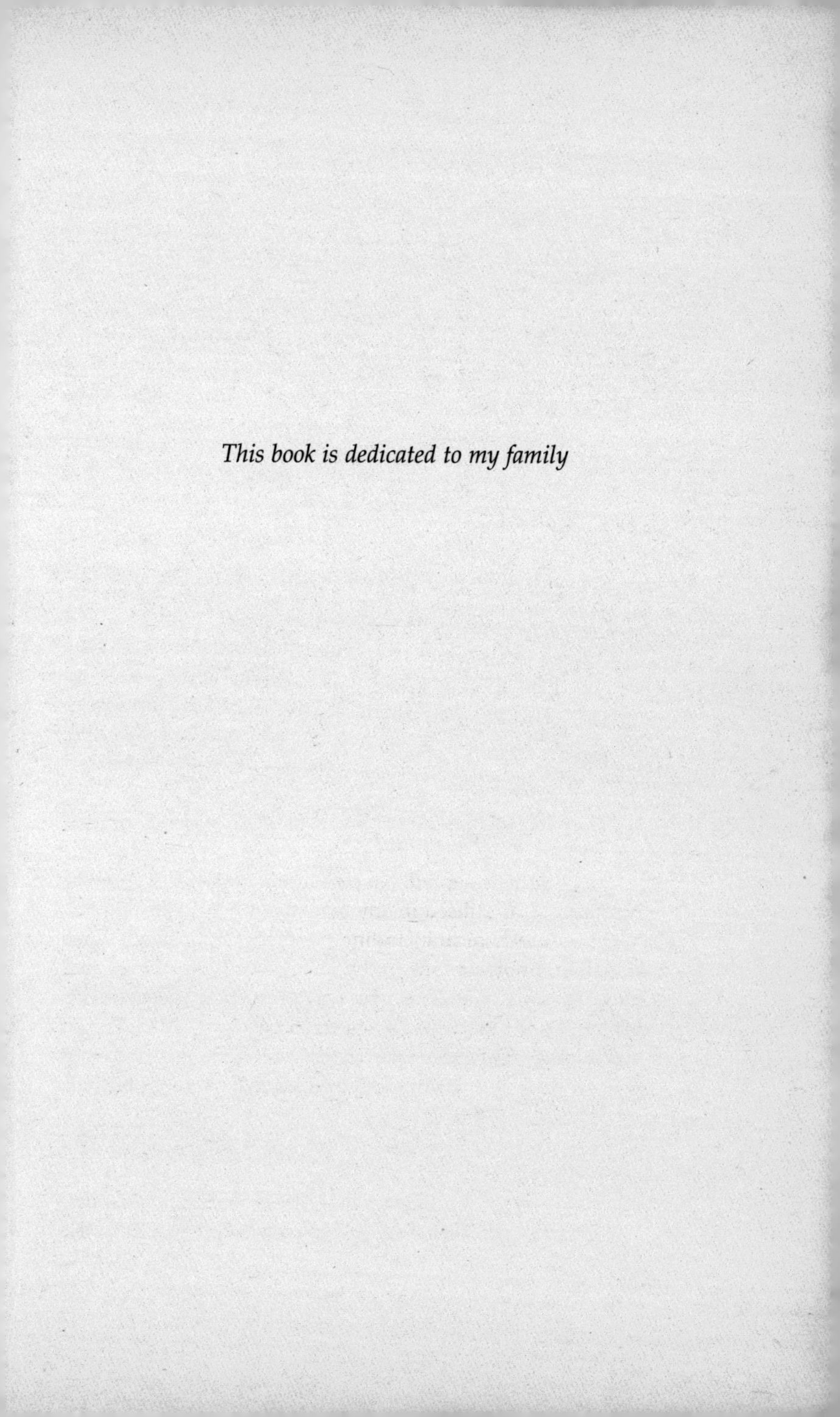

This book is dedicated to my family

acknowledgements

THIS BOOK WOULD not have been possible without the help of a great many people. First and foremost my thanks go to Brendan Anderson for considering me to tell Paddy Grimshaw's life story. Brendan's confidence in me, and outright rejection of any fears I had in my ability to finish what I'd started, led to this book's completion.

I especially want to thank Brendan for his determination in getting this book published following the death of his wife Violet. His generosity of spirit has been an inspiration.

I would also like to thank Damian Keenan for his patience and trust in Brendan's judgment.

A special word of thanks goes of course to the man himself — Paddy Grimshaw — for the hours on end spent reliving both painful and humorous memories. It has been a difficult journey of discovery for Paddy but hopefully the end has at last brought him some of the peace for which he was searching.

To Paddy's worthy confidant, Eddie McCrory, many

thanks for all the lifts, keeping Paddy on track and sharing your memories.

Thanks also to Joe and Gerard Grimshaw for their time, cooperation and tolerance, even with the most mundane of questions.

Thank you to Paddy's friends, Mervyn McWilliams, William Auld, and his former landlady Jenny Bradford.

There were a lot of unanswered questions when Paddy first told me his story. I would like to thank the following people for their kindness in helping to find the answers to many of those questions: to Richard Black, assistant director of disability services at St Luke's Hospital in Armagh; Lynsey Conway at the social witness board office of the Presbyterian Church in Ireland; Beverly Nesbitt, John Misgimmon and Vi Long at the Northern Ireland Institute for the Disabled, formerly Stewart Memorial Home, in Bangor, for a wealth of information, and their time; many thanks to Geri Parker at the Ulster Community and Hospital Trust for her insight into fostering and adoption; the staff at the Linenhall Library in Belfast; the staff at Ormeau Library; the staff at Central Library Newspaper archive; the Public Record Office of Northern Ireland and the Northern Ireland Polio Fellowship. A very special thank you to Eilis Manning and Kathleen McClure from Adopt for their efforts above and beyond the call of duty, for great advice and a friendly ear.

Thanks also to Ann McManus in the *Irish News* photographic department and Jeremy Kirker, the newspaper's chief sub-editor, for his understanding and time off at very little notice.

The challenge of penning your first book is a daunting one and, if it was not for the help and support of friends and family, it would not have been possible.

Thank you to Sarah Kavanagh for her belief in me and constant affirmations before I even had a sentence laid down. A huge thank you to my great friends Ciarda Martin, Lucy Gollogly, Therese McKenna and Laura Semple for endless interruptions, distractions, cups of tea, dragging me out to the pub and words of encouragement to stick with it. This book might have been finished all the sooner without them but it, and I, would have been the worse for it. Thank you all.

Thanks to Brian Semple and Lynne Sharman for ploughing through the first draft and for their suggestions for reworking it, and Tony Bailie for his experience and advice. To my Aunty Kay, who encouraged me to put pen to paper many years ago, and for instilling in me the belief that anything is possible if you put your mind to it.

And finally to my parents, Anne and Vincent, my brothers, Michael and Joseph, for their unknowing inspiration, and my brother and sister, Barry and Martina, for continually asking me, 'Is it finished yet?'

Yes, it is now.

1

IT WAS DARK and musty with a few tiny shards of light stealing their way in through the gaps in the wood. Soft toys surrounded the little boy but they were not intended for his amusement. He had been locked in the toy chest again, and was told he would stay there until he learnt to respect his Gospel. He had forgotten his prayers and had been thrown into the box like a rag doll, and the lid had been slammed firmly shut. It was scary in there, a cramped, dark holding cell for rule-breakers. What if they forgot about him, buried in there under teddy bears with worn-out ears, their soft innards bursting outwards? A tangled mess of shoelaces discarded from old conker duels was strewn across the bottom of the chest, gathering loosely about the ankle of a doll.

Paddy was petrified but he wouldn't let the nurses see that; as far as they were concerned he didn't care. He would do what he wanted, when he wanted. He could hear children's voices, laughter, shouts and excited screams. He didn't want to be in the toy chest any longer. Nine was too young to die, smothered by an avalanche of teddy bears: he wouldn't look so tough then. How long did half an hour last anyway?

Paddy Grimshaw's earliest memories are of the Stewart Memorial Home, more commonly known as the Cripples' Institute, on the Downshire Road in Bangor, County Down. The word 'cripple' was in common parlance at the time and had little of the political incorrectness associated with it today.

'It was all right at the start at the home, but it was later on, when I got a wee bit older and started to get obstreperous, that all the business started with the cupboards and the toy chest,' Paddy recalls.

Situated on the scenic Down coast, Stewart Memorial was one of three detached houses on the Stricklands site that were known in the 1940s as the Homes of Rest. The redbrick Victorian buildings sat in beautiful grounds, perched on the top of a hill, with lawns spilling down onto the shores of Belfast Lough. The Cripples' Home was founded by a Christian family at the beginning of the twentieth century to alleviate the suffering of the poor who worked tortuously long hours in Belfast's mills and factories. John Brown, the Lord Mayor of Belfast in 1878, was a unionist councillor and dedicated philanthropist. He and his two brothers undertook relief works and started mission halls for the working class. Brown's daughter continued her father's charitable work after her marriage to A W Vance of Mornington, Bangor. In 1890 the Home of Rest for Women and Girls was opened to provide respite for mothers and children.

Eight years later, plans were drawn up for a separate

Men's Home of Rest on the Stricklands property. When work was complete it was used as a holiday home, and to nurse soldiers who had returned from the Boer War. The homes proved to be a major success but, in the opinion of the Vance family, there was still much more work to be done in tackling social and economic injustices. The sight of disabled children hobbling around Belfast's streets tore at their heart-strings, and fundraising began in earnest to open 'a home for cripples' on the Stricklands grounds. And so the Cripples' Home was born.

It was here that Paddy Grimshaw came to live five years after his birth, ushered out into the world alone as a 'wee abandoned', discarded by his mother.

A black-haired, blue-eyed baby at birth, Patrick Joseph Grimshaw took his first gulps of air as the horrific events of World War II were drawing to a close. A few days after he was born, on 4 September 1944, the anti-air-raid blackout precautions across Northern Ireland were relaxed. The atmosphere was tangibly lighter as the world tended to its wounds and people dared to hope the end of war was nigh. In a small house at Catherine Court in south Belfast, Paddy was brought into the world, greeted by Mary Dunn. Little is known about Mrs Dunn other than she lived at this address with her husband Patrick. Whether she was a mid-wife or a friend of Paddy's mother, Philomena, is uncertain. Where Paddy spent the earliest years of his life also remains a mystery.

On 9 September 1949 he was transferred to Stewart Memorial from the nursery at the City Hospital in Belfast. Paddy had spent the previous nine months at the hospital receiving treatment for poliomyelitis, otherwise known as infantile paralysis or more commonly, polio. He had contracted the ailment in December 1948. Polio is a highly infectious disease which spreads quickly from person to person, usually orally through food or water contaminated with faeces. The virus travels down to the intestinal lining where it passes into the blood. Once the virus begins its assault on the central nervous system, paralysis can occur in a matter of hours. Polio can strike at any age but the majority of cases are in children aged between three and five. The flu-like symptoms include fatigue, fever, vomiting, headache and stiffness in the neck and limbs. The strain of the virus Paddy caught that Christmas invaded his spinal cord where it targeted the central nervous system, spreading along nerve fibres. As the virus multiplied, it destroyed the motor neurons which activated his body muscles. Once the neurons are destroyed they cannot be regenerated and affected muscles can no longer function. Polio can lead to paralysis, most commonly in the legs, rendering the affected limbs into floppy, lifeless pieces of muscle. Extreme infection can also lead to paralysis of the trunk, the thorax and the abdomen. However, only one in two hundred infections actually led to irreversible paralysis. In the late 1930s, and throughout the 1940s, children in Northern Ireland were particularly susceptible to the disease. Between 1938 and 1949 there were 417 cases of polio in the north. From the end of 1948 to the end of 1949, when Paddy's young body was struggling to keep the infection at bay, there were more than fifty cases. The following year the number rose to a staggering 272. Paddy has no recollection of the disease taking hold of his body, overpowering it with waves of sickness, fever and muscle-aches while he battled to reject it. His fight was in vain. He survived but the virus ravaged his legs, robbing him of his healthy limbs. He was left with a weakened left leg, which had to be encased in an iron calliper, and a lower right leg reliant on a knee iron for support.

Four months before Paddy was delivered into the hands of Stewart Memorial, the welfare department at the City Hospital sent a letter to the home from Dr Hall, the doctor who had been overseeing Paddy's treatment. Dr Hall recommended Paddy as a prospective resident at the Cripples' Institute, as he was out of danger and nothing more could be done for him in hospital with the exception of monthly examinations and remedial exercises. There was no mention of Paddy being returned home to his mother. Whether Philomena Grimshaw had ever nursed her sick son is not known. In the application form from the hospital, dated 4 May 1949, which requested Paddy's admission to the Incorporated Cripples' Institute, his mother was listed as his nearest living relative but no address was given. The only other information about Paddy's background was his religion: he was listed as Roman Catholic. Dr Thomas Hanna's medical report on the same document confirms that Paddy had been known to him for six months and he'd been an inmate at Ava Hospital within the Belfast City Hospital complex.

Young Paddy was oblivious to the efforts being made to find him a home where he could recuperate and begin adjusting to life. On 21 May the General Secretary of Stewart Memorial Home wrote to the Director of Education in Belfast asking if the Authority would accept financial responsibility for Paddy. The committee agreed and, on 9 September 1949, four days after his fifth birthday, Paddy became part of the Stewart Memorial Home family. He shared his new home with twenty-four other children in accommodation divided into two dormitories, one for the girls and one for the boys. Paddy recalls a nurse telling him that he was four years and three months old when he caught the crippling disease.

'Sister Brady in the City Hospital — where we used to go to orthopaedic outpatients—always maintained that I was about that age when I took polio,' he says. 'I never remember walking ordinary at all. I can always remember wearing callipers. I never remember being without them.'

In so many ways Paddy has 'never walked ordinary'. Left alone in the world, he had to make his own way in order to survive. Having as a toddler mastered the art of walking, Paddy had to relearn how to propel himself forward; but this time he had steel scaffolding to contend with — unyielding and unbending, especially at the knees. He couldn't quite get his young mind around the reason why his legs didn't cooperate the way they once had. The doctors had been fussing over him, always poking and prodding at his legs, so he knew there was something wrong — just what, he couldn't figure out. He knew he was telling his limbs to move but he just couldn't rouse them. It was infuriating. The only obvious explanation was those horrible iron things they strapped to him every day. They made his legs feel alien. But no matter how hard he tried, he couldn't walk without them. If they were so insistent that he wore them, he was going to have to learn to walk with them, and with no loving, attentive mother to hold his small hands and encourage him. His first fall was met with strong arms swiftly returning him to his polio-wizened feet, where he was made to try again and again until he got it right. Casting his mind back to how he reacted to this walking malarkey, he is philosophical about the whole affair.

'Like everybody else, I think I fell and that was a good experience for me. But the thing was I got up again. It was very difficult but we eventually got there through sheer determination and stubbornness.'

The stilted walk of the calliper-wearer is not conducive to speed. Without being able to bend at the knee, each step is slow and exaggerated. First the calliper-laden child had to master the art of balancing on one leg, then pulling the other leg through — weighted down by the heavy calliper — in one steady swing, while simultaneously shifting balance from the back leg to the front, carrying the back leg across the gulf created and stamping it on the ground while holding his balance. It was a slow and frustrating progress, and not one Paddy enjoyed.

'It was as if I had two artificial legs,' he says. 'The callipers were reasonably heavy and I wore big surgical boots with tubing at the sides for the callipers. I sort of swung into it. As I gradually got used to the callipers, I was able to move along with more speed but I fell a lot at the start.'

The staff, however, thought it better to show little or no sympathy for Paddy and the other children as they made their faltering way.

'They thought they were doing good for me. It was the Christian thing. They thought the Lord was going to save everybody with a miracle, but unfortunately it didn't work out that way. I know you have to be a believer but,' he says with a laugh, 'I just remember crying and being very bad-tempered. I think I was just an awkward child under the circumstances.'

Children grew to detest their callipers. Their frustration at not being able to walk, as 'normal' children did, was taken out on the very tools that were facilitating what limited mobility they had.

'I couldn't get them off quick enough at night. It still happens until this day: a lot of polios (Paddy's synonym for polio survivors) will tell you about callipers. The awkwardness of them, so cumbersome, and I saw other children walking about ordinary without anything. Without them, I was able to get around but I had to hold on to something.'

Paddy became a regular visitor with the orthopaedic doctors at the City Hospital, where they assessed his progress with walking aids and put him through gruelling physiotherapy sessions. As they adjusted his callipers, they assured him this was all intended to help him to walk better. While he enjoyed the fuss the friendly nurses and doctors were making of him, he wished they would one day take off his 'manacles' and tell him he was free to walk unfettered.

Paddy's long-time friend, Eddie McCrory, himself a polio survivor, also served his time with callipers and says they were never an easy contraption to get the hang of.

'When I was young, when I sat down my leg just jutted out straight,' says Eddie. 'Then they become more modern, and they had these locks so that when you sat down, you could take the locks off and bend your knee. You couldn't walk with them unlocked. When I first had them, there was a pull on them, a strap, and you pulled it and it released the lock. If somebody pulled the leather as a joke, then you just went down, because you hadn't the strength to keep your knee straight. There was also a strap around the shoe and that made them much more noticeable.'

Eddie contracted polio when he was five. He was determined that he wouldn't be dependent on callipers for the rest of his life, so, at the tender age of seven, he took matters into his own hands and began working on a plan to rid himself of the despised metal frames.

'You know how I got rid of mine?' he shares with a self-satisfied smile. 'I had the two callipers and I used to have a brace on my back. When I went to bed I had to sleep in a mould of myself with bandages wrapped around me. There were two beds in the room and I would try to walk from bed to bed without the callipers. The next thing, I would be on the ground with a thump and couldn't get up. Then my mother and father would come up. Once I hit the metal bit of the bed and chipped my knee, so I was in plaster for six weeks. I remember that the orthopaedic surgeon went bananas.

'My mother told me that I was responsible for getting rid of my callipers. I said to the surgeon — I was only seven — I said, "The day I get this plaster-cast off I'll be trying that again." Then my mother and father started holding my arms so at least they would catch me. I actually chipped my bone again about six weeks after that and I was in plaster for another six weeks. But by the time I was eight I had no callipers.'

This shared glory is an important one to polio survivors, who are set the challenge from the day they take their first steps to aspire to walk like the able-bodied people around them. It is entirely dependent on the progression of the disease, and how it affects each individual's limbs, as to how well they meet this challenge. Eddie's single-minded intent to survive without callipers was a personal coup supported by loving parents. For Paddy, however, his carers did not have the time to give him the undivided attention necessary to wean him off his callipers and he was to endure them for many years to come.

'In those days we also had wooden crutches that everybody used. If the children fell, then the nurses would give them a tap over the head with a stick.'

Paddy laughs now at this treatment but not all of the memories at the Cripples' Institute are recalled with the same light-heartedness. As a Christian home, residents at Stewart Memorial had to attend Gospel meetings regularly. These meetings were not restricted to the home and, because it didn't have its own transport, the children would often have to walk miles to get to them. The tortuous journey to the meetings with unforgiving callipers is something Paddy recalls with chagrin.

'The thing I really hated about the home in Bangor was that you got dragged around to the Pickie Pool (an open-air salt-water swimming pool and leisure area) to the meetings. I think that is where I got my temper from. Even to this very day I'm very highly strung. Somebody was always pulling me, saying, "You're going to this meeting." And that was every darn week. It was a fairly long walk. It would have taken me a good hour, and it was tiring. I hated it. In those days I had the two callipers, one large calliper and then the wee half one on the other leg. I used to get very annoyed and the nurses would hold my hand and say, "Come on now." There were no electric wheelchairs in those days.'

Being coerced into doing things he found physically and mentally challenging fired up a defiant spirit in Paddy. This resilient and determined attitude is one that sits well with him, even now. His once-black hair has long turned grey. He now sports a short-cropped crew-cut style which belies his toughness. Reliant on an electric wheelchair, Paddy is short in height but thickly set. He has a wheezy laugh that thunders up his throat and explodes into the room, shaking his sturdy shoulders and infecting all those around him with its warmth. It was upon these sturdy shoulders that Paddy sometimes felt the world was resting its woes. Having spent his life within the confines of the social care system, tossed from pillar to post, from one home to another, Paddy never had the luxury of enjoying family life. Stewart Memorial gave him his introduction into the world and was the closest thing to a family he was to experience for another fifty years. The defiance he learnt there stood him in good stead for the trials life was to throw at him.

'The beauty about the home in Bangor was that everybody was in the same boat with different disabilities. The only time it really annoyed me was when I was going to church on a Sunday with my short trousers on and my callipers and people were looking at me. That was the biggest problem — embarrassment and shyness. They were just staring. Kids do it today. "Mister, why are you in that wheelchair?" they ask. Just the other day I heard a wee boy saying, "Mommy, mommy, you see that man there, he can't walk", and his mum said, "Yeah, he needs a special rotovator." And I said to myself, where did that woman get that word from? Another man says to me in Ballyclare, "Mister, how much would one of those electric wheelchairs cost? I could be doing with one of them." Well, I said, "Sir, if you have a spare £4,000, I'll get you one." He says, "Ah, it doesn't matter, I'll keep on walking."'

Paddy only wishes it was so easy to shrug off his dependency on his wheelchair. Ironically, as the years have passed, he has finally been able to wave goodbye to his callipers as they gave way to his four-wheeled friend. When he was a child he didn't anticipate that getting what he wanted would actually feel so much like losing even more.

He doesn't miss his callipers so much, as what they enabled him to do — walk where and when he wanted, in his own way. In his younger years Paddy wasn't given the option of walking his own way. There was a system and people to be obeyed. Life in the Cripples' Institute necessitated a controlled and strict environment, governed by rules and routine. It was a way of life that everyone without exception had to get used to.

'It was very regimental in a sense. You were sort of made to do things. The general manager, Jim Dornan, ruled the roost. He was in his forties, very sturdy. He was very, very strict. I didn't like him much. He lived up the road a bit and he could come from his back garden into the home. But we wouldn't have seen him that much every day.

'The principal was Miss Gilpin — of the Gilpins' clothing business family. She was a very tall lady with black hair — quite good looking. On the whole she wasn't too bad,' Paddy recalls. 'The under-matron was the Reverend Carson's sister — Miss Carson, we called her — and then there were the nurses after that. Some of the nurses were nice.

'Every day was the same, the same chores. As soon as we got up in the morning, before we got any breakfast at all, there was a wee prayer meeting. That was the routine. For breakfast you would have got cornflakes, toast or porridge; you would never have had eggs or anything like that. And after breakfast we'd play with toys. In the afternoon — the school wasn't there at the start — you just pottered about. It became very repetitive and very strict. But I had good times in it too. It was good old craic,' he hastens to add. 'We bathed in these huge baths, the biggest I'd ever seen in my life. But when you got a bit older you didn't want to get undressed for the nurses to bathe you.'

On 31 October 1952 Miss Gilpin received a letter from the Macosquin Girls' Auxiliary in Bushtown, Coleraine. The letter contained an inquiry from the group's secretary, Jamie Mitchell, over the possibility of the branch 'adopting' an orphan cripple. Miss Mitchell asserted the enthusiasm of the ten girls in her branch at the prospect of helping a child in the home's charge. At the bottom of the letter, where Miss Mitchell had signed off, Paddy Grimshaw's name was written to the side in Miss Gilpin's handwriting with a question mark beside it. Unbeknown to Paddy, who had just turned eight, Miss Gilpin was to suggest him as the perfect candidate for sponsorship. Miss Gilpin hastily passed the Girls' Auxiliary's request on to Mr T J Rainsford, the General Secretary of the Incorporated Cripples' Institute in Wellington Place, Belfast. Within five days of receiving the letter Mr Rainsford replied to Miss Mitchell, expressing his appreciation for the group's interest in adopting a child. He proffered Paddy as the child who would benefit most from their involvement. He wrote:

'There is one lad at present in our special school at Bangor, Paddy Grimshaw, aged eight years, who has neither father nor mother. As a result of infantile paralysis at a very early age, he suffers from a considerable degree of paralysis to both legs and can only get about by the use of crutches along with steel callipers to support his legs. This would seem to me to be the child who could benefit most by the interest of the members of your branch. I realise that it would probably be quite impossible for members of your branch to visit Paddy very often but he certainly would appreciate a visit ... Such visits could be followed by a letter from whoever had made the visit and I know that occasional gifts would probably also be appreciated by Paddy.

'As you will see there are no definite rules which can be laid down regarding this, but I feel if your branch decides to go ahead with the arrangement that time and experience will indicate many ways in which this particular child can be helped.'

It was more than a month before Mr Rainsford received a decision from Macosquin. Miss Mitchell replied by writing:

'The decision to adopt Paddy Grimshaw was unanimous. We all appreciate the sympathetic consideration you have given to our request and we are looking forward to helping Paddy in the future. I should warn you that you will probably be inundated with questions about him.'

In early January 1953, Mr Rainsford visited the Macosquin Auxiliary branch in Coleraine to give a talk on the work of the Cripples' Institutes. While there he furnished the group with a picture of Paddy which Miss Mitchell promised to hang in the branch's session room.

One month after Mr Rainsford's visit to Paddy's new benefactors, Paddy was rushed into the City Hospital with abdominal pain. He was no stranger to hospital with his regular orthopaedic sessions. In fact, he was usually delighted to escape the home for a couple of hours and to have doctors and nurses fussing over him. However, it was quite another thing to be sent to the City screaming in agony with a searing pain in his side. The doctors diagnosed him with a suspected appendicular abscess. Swiftly taken into theatre, he was operated on immediately and the abscess drained but his appendix was not removed. The surgery was a success but Paddy's temperature failed to return to normal despite a course of drugs being administered. This proved to be a worry to the doctors; his medication was duly changed and he eventually improved. He spent forty-eight days in hospital in all from the date of his admission in February until he was deemed fit enough to be discharged in April.

Paddy's new guardians made their first trip from Coleraine to Stewart Memorial to visit him in July 1953. It was well worth the wait, as Miss Mitchell informed Mr Rainsford in writing on 30 July. In her letter she included a photograph she had taken of Paddy during the visit. She was overjoyed at having finally met him and profusely thanked Mr Rainsford for accommodating their visit:

'I must say thank you for your kindness in showing us round the home. The girls were all very pleased to hear that we had seen Paddy and are looking forward to the next GA session when we will be having our meetings with his photograph looking down at us — very different from the usual crowd of past ministers and members of session.'

Miss Mitchell must have been unaware that, shortly after her meeting with Paddy, he had once again been taken into hospital. This time he was on a waiting list to have his appendix removed. He was admitted on 22 July and three days later he was taken to the theatre for his appendicectomy. There were no complications with the operation, but Paddy, always one for the limelight, conjured up a little drama when he came round after the surgery. Curious to see how the doctors had patched him up again, he decided to take a sneaky look at the new scar on his stomach but inadvertently reopened the wound.

'I remember pulling the plaster off to have a look. I had to be rushed back into theatre again with the big mask put across my face to put me out.'

Paddy had learned from an early age that he could attract attention by fanning the flames of any situation to prolong the furore. Starved of the affection parents afford to their children, by creating a commotion he ensured that he was noticed and attended to by his carers for however brief a period. When his hospital drama had ended, and he had been firmly instructed not to touch his bandages again, he settled down for his month-long stay at the City.

Interestingly, between his first and second admissions to the City, Paddy appears to have undergone a conversion. Despite his Catholic origins, he had been brought up as a Protestant. On his initial visit to the hospital his religion was listed as Baptist, but by his return, a mere five months later, he had converted to Church of Ireland.

On the road to recovery Paddy was discharged from hospital on 18 August and returned to Stewart Memorial. He had realised for some time that he was no ordinary boy. Hurdles faced him and, hampered by his condition, they were not easy to overcome. This realisation, and the consequential frustration, led Paddy to do what would be seen today as 'acting out' but was regarded by the home's nurses as simply disruptive behaviour that would not be tolerated. He kicked out against the home's regime and aired feelings of oppression which he could not quite understand himself.

'I was a very obstreperous, very hard child. I was very disruptive, hard to handle,' he admits.

As his behaviour worsened the staff decided something had to be done. In January 1954 Paddy was sent to an educational psychologist at the Child Guidance Clinic in the Royal Victoria Hospital on Belfast's Falls Road. As if on cue, Paddy performed well for the white-coated lady. She found him to be a quiet and pleasant child with a lower than average IQ. Her analysis was that Paddy's institutionalisation and the limited environment of the home were major contributing factors to his level of intelligence and behaviour. Her report stated:

'This boy was very quiet but little emotional tension was apparent. He was cheerful and cooperative and gave straightforward responses to test questions. His basal age was 6:0 with scatter only to 7 in which he completed only two tests. This very limited scatter is probably due to institutional background and necessarily limited environment.'

Armed with this information, the staff had an explanation for why Paddy became so easily exasperated and in turn disobedient, but this was of little aid in actually helping them prevent his outbursts. In an effort to rein in the increasingly uncontrollable Paddy, they resorted to imprisoning him in a toy chest when he was particularly difficult.

'It was a big long box full of toys and, if I misbehaved or anything, they'd put me in it for half an hour to make me see the error of my ways,' Paddy recalls, his jovial tone initially belying any feeling of fear. 'But that was sort of frightening, you know,' he adds, his eyes taking on a distant look, as though he has been transported back to his nine-year-old self, trapped in the dark and claustrophobic trunk. 'I just sat in it with all the soft toys and the lid was put down. It was dark. It was scary. I can't understand to this day why they'd do that sort of thing to me. Why would they put me in a box when I misbehaved?'

It is no wonder then that Paddy loved to escape the home to the freedom of the City and the hospital's caring orthopaedic staff for check-ups on his progress with his callipers.

The undivided attention he received from the doctors and nurses was a complete contrast to that of the home where he was one of a large group of children, all with challenging demands. He felt special when he was in hospital, parading up and down for the doctor with his callipers on, bending his legs this way and that. The doctor was only interested in what Paddy could do, nobody else. For an hour at least he was important. The doctors closely monitored Paddy's walking, doing everything in their power to make his steps easier and more fluid.

A vaccine for polio had still to be found and, as scientists battled to produce one, the disease continued to ravage children across the world. The orthopaedic staff working with Paddy continued to fight valiantly to correct the limbs weakened by the disease.

In early January 1954 Paddy attended the City for remedial therapy. The doctor who examined him recorded in his notes that Paddy was walking a little better, although he was still 'hitching up' his shoulders. His right leg was good and his quadriceps were improving but he also noted that the toes on both feet were overlapping. Scholls separators had been used to straighten his toes but were unsuccessful. Three months later, Paddy was examined by Dr Hall who recommended that he see a specialist from England with a view to being fitted with new callipers. As the summer holidays approached Paddy was given a set of brand new, long callipers. When he returned to see Dr Gregg in November 1954, ten-year-old Paddy was walking very well.

William Auld was placed in Stewart Memorial in 1955, aged

seven. Almost five years Paddy's junior, he remembers him as one of the bigger boys who was always getting into trouble.

'There was what they called the big boys' room and the small boys' room and Paddy was in the big boys' room. I know there was one time when the head, Mr Dornan, had to come over and calm him down. Because he was older, he wasn't in our gang. I don't think we were too friendly at school, it was more recently that happened.'

Luckily for William he never shared Paddy's experience of the toy box.

'If we did anything wrong we were sent upstairs to the physiotherapist's room right at the top of the building because it was only used twice a week. We had to learn twenty verses from the Bible and we had to go down and recite these word-perfect before we were cleansed,' William laughs. 'Religion was pumped into you day and night. We had prayers in the morning and prayers at night. Sunday — off to church and then prayers again that night. No TV, except when *Songs of Praise* (a televised religious programme) was on from Bangor.'

Unlike Paddy, William came from a stable family who took advantage of the home to assist with his recovery and for some relief from full-time care. He contracted polio at eighteen months of age, as did his sister, who made a full recovery. William left hospital when he was four, going home to parents who were unprepared to cope with a polio-ridden child who could not walk or do much for himself.

'They didn't know what they were going to do with me when I got out of hospital. But there used to be a programme on the radio — Wilford Pickles — it was like a musical hour, and he collected money for charity. He gave money to the Cripples' Institute, who ran the Cripples' Home, and Miss Gilpin from the home brought me out this train set donated by Wilford Pickles. I thought this was great. She introduced my parents to the home and they thought it would be a good idea for me to move down there.'

There had previously been no formal education at Stewart Memorial and it was with the advent of the school that parents of children with disabilities sent their offspring to board.

When the school was introduced Miss Gilpin also took on the role of teacher. This was to be Paddy's first brush with formal education.

'It was actually in the home. You went down a corridor to it from the dining room. Miss Gilpin was the teacher. We didn't have a school uniform,' he recalls. 'School went on from about ten o'clock in the morning until two in the afternoon, so I didn't learn all that much. I did multiplication and decimals and all that sort of thing — just the basics. I never remember doing an exam. I have never taken an exam in my life.'

As to whether he was a good student, Paddy shrugs, laughs and says simply, 'Not really.'

William agrees that the curriculum at Stewart Memorial did little to enhance his education.

'We didn't really learn that much at it, mainly because we were in and out of hospital. I didn't really learn anything until I left there. I didn't end up hating it the way Paddy did. It didn't advance my education but it did advance many other aspects of my life.'

Paddy had little interest in learning and, as with his behaviour outside the classroom, he didn't take kindly to being told to sit still at his desk. His tantrums remained very much a part of life in the home irrespective of the punishment the nurses and the matron dished out. He was often reprimanded with a spell in the toy box for forgetting his prayers and this caused him no end of frustration. To compound that, there were Gospel meetings to be attended.

'There were a lot of Gospel meetings, from morning to night; that was the problem too,' he says.

Although Paddy hated being pulled to and from the meetings, these actually brought structure to his young life. Through his forced attendance, the angst-ridden child discovered he had a talent that neither he nor his carers could have anticipated.

'Every other day we went to a meeting and we were traipsed round the back road to Bangor. That was to sing hymns. It was an open-air Gospel meeting and the public were there. The meetings lasted quite a long time. But once we got there and settled down it was great craic, it calmed us down. I really enjoyed it. They used to get barber shop choirboys in and they were quite good. But there was still that strictness there: if you didn't behave you got a skelp across the backside. It sharpened you up.

'But the singing made me feel sort of great. I thought I was a star and I was going to make it to the top. I could always sing, from day one. I remember singing on the radio one time when the Gospel meeting was broadcast. I always used to sing.'

Singing was a release for Paddy which, temporarily at least, quietened his rage and gave him a sense of purpose and pride. He was on top of the world when his lungs filled with air and his voice flowed out, fulfilling a primal urge to be heard and understood, to connect with those around him.

It was a precious moment, sharing something with the appreciative and joyful faces of the crowd. Religion became a seminal part of Paddy's life in the home. It came to represent a medley of emotions: frustration at having to hobble along to meetings, fear of being reprimanded for failing to learn prayers adequately, and the joy and freedom that singing brought.

'The first church service I went to was the Life Boys (a section of the Boys' Brigade) round where the big cinema was in Bangor. It was a Baptist church. I used to see them getting dunked, as I used to call it, to baptise them. But after that I didn't go there anymore. The rest of us joined the First Presbyterian Church in Bangor. I remember we had to wear short grey trousers, a black blazer, a tie and a white shirt.'

As a member of the First Presbyterian Church, Paddy joined the Boys' Brigade (BB) in 1956. This was another regimented organisation with Christianity at its heart.

But it was in the BB that Paddy found yet another outlet for release. There were Bible classes to be attended but also drill parades, which he adored. He was a part of something bigger, something outside the home, a new gang of boys — and he loved it. It was here too that he met a teenager whom he idolised, and who later became a hero on the Northern Ireland soccer scene.

'The BB was a different ball game. It stiffened you up a bit. I was interested in the sports.

'Terry Neill was my squad captain. He put me on the straight and narrow. He was a couple of years older than me. We used to go away to a place in England called Staines, in Middlesex, for camping. It was a big squad but I can't remember anybody besides myself who was disabled.'

Ironically, Paddy grew to love the order that the BB

brought to his life. While he was obviously different, he made friends with able-bodied boys who accepted him as one of the gang without question.

'I enjoyed the discipline about it. There was good company, everybody was friendly and we got away on holidays.'

Inspired by Terry Neill and his sporting talent, Paddy's interest in soccer grew and with it the desire to live as a normal boy who would one day grow up to be a footballer.

'When he was my squad captain he was centre-half for Bangor. I remember going to see him a couple of times. We weren't really allowed to go to football matches. I used to watch them and think, how do they do that? When you were disabled you couldn't do it.'

But Paddy wouldn't be put off. It was out on to the lawn at Stewart Memorial with a football and crutches under both armpits. A blind eye was often turned to the illegal use of the crutches during the match. Creating their own special blend of football and hockey, the children were hooked. They had their own approach to the sport and it was all the more fun for it.

'I played with the crutches and walking sticks. I fell more times than enough,' he remembers with a laugh. 'We used to play with Jim Dornan's son and hit the ball with the sticks. We didn't care.

'In the home I'd say, "I'd love to be one of those footballers or a goalkeeper." We used to play in the BB and I tried my best. They helped you along, they didn't patronise you. But in later life, it struck me what I couldn't do when I had to make my own way, what I wasn't capable of doing no matter how badly I wanted it.'

Terry Neill went on to play for and captain both Arsenal

and Northern Ireland. During his time on the Northern Ireland squad Terry played alongside football legend George Best. Paddy's and George's paths were to cross later in life at the peak of George's career, and the two would develop a mutual respect for their individual talents.

Despite his realisation that he would never make it as a footballer, the game inspired him — but not always for the best. In his early teens Paddy grew more and more fond of testing the boundaries and the patience of the staff at the home. Going to football matches was frowned upon. But one day, fuelled by the desire to see a game, Paddy decided to defy the home's rules and go AWOL for a while. Roping in a couple of accomplices, he and his friends set off. Unbeknown to Paddy, one of his trusted sidekicks had a plan of his own which involved going AWOL on a permanent basis.

'We weren't allowed out of the home to go into Bangor on our own. It was the same with football matches. Well, we were standing at the bus stop, we were on our way to the match and the next thing O'Sullivan took off and we couldn't find him. He absconded,' Paddy remembers with a laugh.

Undeterred by his runaway pal, Paddy remained determined to make it to the match, regardless. He had come this far and he was adamant that he wasn't going home without seeing the game.

'We got to the football match and I said, "Don't worry about it until we get back." I don't know if they ever got him again. He wasn't in the home all that long before he ran off. But I think we got in trouble for that — maybe lost a meal or something, but it was a good old laugh in those days.'

To children like Paddy, who did not often receive gifts or

have much to call their own, the smallest possessions were prized. So it was with glee and much pride that Paddy became the owner of his first and very own 'smart' shirt, one he had been admiring for some time.

'Beside our Boys' Brigade premises there was a men's clothing shop and I used to admire all the clothes in it. I was in my wee grey shorts all the time and hadn't the money to buy anything. There was a lovely shirt. It was pink and it was really modern. I got it one day. I don't know how, the staff must have bought it for me. It was top of the range then. It was the Teddy boy age and we used to try to get our drain-pipe trousers on over callipers so we could stand outside Barry's Amusements with Brylcreem in our hair. I was still young. On Friday night we would stand there — a crowd of boys from the BB and a couple from the home — chewing gum and looking round us.'

Fitting in with the 'normal' lads in Bangor gave Paddy a sense of confidence as he strutted his stuff around the town, looking good and feeling like a 'normal' lad himself. These were days Paddy seized on and enjoyed every second of. However, when Miss Gilpin found out about the 'boys about town' she soon put a stop to it.

'I bought the drain-pipes myself, unbeknown to the home. They didn't know I had them.

'I smuggled them in. I saved up. We used to have a green book like a war ration book and I saved my pocket money every week, so I went and bought the drain-pipes. We were real poseurs. It used to be good craic. But it didn't last too long, someone must have squealed. When Miss Gilpin found out, she said, "Get those things off you. You're not wearing them in a respectable home like this." That was the end of that. Whatever happened to them I don't know, whether she confiscated them or what. I think they might have ended up in one of the fires I was lighting in the mornings.'

It wasn't long before his precious pink shirt met a similar fate to that of his drain-pipes.

'I was lighting the fire at the home one morning and the flames caught the cuff of the shirt. I caught it in time but I had to get it off quick. I wasn't burnt but the shirt was ruined. I could have cried.'

Paddy's rebellious streak continued as he embarked on what would be a lifelong career as a smoker.

'The first time I ever tried to smoke I rolled up a bit of hard toilet paper,' the forty-a-day man says, beginning to laugh. 'Me and another bloke put a light to it but when I went to inhale it nearly killed me. I think Miss Gilpin must have smelt it because we weren't long putting it down the toilet.'

It was to be a few years before Paddy was to taste his first proper cigarette. He admits now he savoured each delicious draw. Luckily for Paddy, when he landed his first job, his pay packet was not to be depleted by surreptitiously forking out for cigarettes. Without a family to spend the holidays with, he was eager to explore the world outside the home and assert his independence. So when the offer of a summer job came up he didn't hesitate in going for it. The position was in a potato crisp factory, owned by the Smith family of Bangor.

'I did general labouring, putting the crisps on the conveyor belt, washing the floors — a dogsbody really. The smell of the place with crisps was terrible. I was allowed to eat as much as I wanted but after a few days I was sick of them.'

In order to get to work Paddy had to use a disabled person's bicycle/wheelchair which he sat in and propelled using a pedal powered by hand. While not exactly the Alps in terms of its mountainous regions, Bangor still had enough hills to be daunting to a young disabled lad unused to the roads and the seemingly gravitational pull of all things towards Bangor marina. The dark forces of fate were to lead this intrepid explorer to an unexpected destination.

'When I was coming down the hill in Bangor, the oul' chain broke and I ended up in a flower pot in the middle of the roundabout.'

Helped to his feet by a passer-by who mended his chain, Paddy, armed with his dented ego, made his way slowly back to the home.

'When I arrived back Miss Gilpin says to me, "What happened to you?" So I got reprimanded for that. I was a tough old cookie in my day.'

William Auld has his own memories of life as a boarder at Stewart Memorial. He joined the boys in their dormitory on the first floor of the home. Unfortunately for the girls they had another flight of stairs to scale before they reached their dormitory on the second floor.

'I was always glad that because of our disabilities the boys had to climb up only one flight of stairs,' William says. 'Because I was fat then, I used to break my callipers a lot. I couldn't walk at all. I had no strength at all. Once I did get callipers, walking about with the weight of me, my heels were starting to turn in. The first operation I had corrected that and then two years later the same thing happened again. This time they put pins into the shoes. Certainly everybody else that was there could get around better than I could. About ninety percent of my body was affected, whereas Paddy had two good arms. I couldn't use a wheelchair. With one arm it is very hard to steer a wheelchair, so anytime I was out, I was in a pushchair.'

A bit of roguish behaviour on William's part led him to have his own near brush with death.

'I remember one time going from Bangor West into Bangor along the coast. It's an up and down walk. I remember the nurses taking us out for an hour. We stopped at the top of a hill and I thought it would be good fun to let the brake off. I went rolling down the hill and one of the nurses caught me just in time. I could have ended up in the sea.'

William was very much at the mercy of the nurses and reliant upon them for manoeuvring him about the home. There was no lift in Stewart Memorial when he began boarding but it was thanks to him that the home ushered in a new era in 1958 by raising funds to have one installed.

'As I said, I was very fat then because I couldn't exercise and I had no callipers, so I piled on the beef. They had this electric chair that had three cogs on it and it was able to go up the stairs though somebody had to pull it up.'

While the lift was a great addition to the home it did not erase the fact that Paddy and William's ability to walk was severely hampered. Paddy's toes were bent over one another, making it almost impossible to put weight on them without experiencing excruciating pain. On 16 September 1958, the fourteen-year-old Paddy was seen by Dr Baker, an orthopaedic surgeon at the City Hospital. Dr Baker was keen that Paddy have surgery to correct his feet and recommended that he attend Musgrave Park Hospital to have the procedures.

'The pain in my feet was unbearable. At the City Hospital, Sister Brady said to me, "Within a fortnight you'll be in getting your operation." And she was absolutely right, not long to wait compared to now.'

As Paddy had no relatives to give consent for the surgery Miss Gilpin forwarded her approval for the treatment. On 27 October he was admitted to Musgrave along with William Auld and David McMullan, who were also to have surgery. The corrective surgery Paddy required was quite severe.

'In those days they had to break the toes and then put pins in them to keep them straight. I was in hospital for three to four months which was a long time to be kept by today's standards.'

Paddy has vivid memories of one very distinctive surgeon who operated on him during his stay in Musgrave. 'Hairy' Osterberg used to come into pre-op to reassure patients.

'He was so hairy. He had hair the whole way down his arms and coming out over his shirt from his chest. He was bald on the top of his head but had hair around the sides. He was a good surgeon,' Paddy adds as if by way of consolation.

Paddy thoroughly enjoyed his stay at Musgrave, surrounded by friendly nurses and his pair of pals from Stewart Memorial.

'They were good days, even though I had the operations. There was an old guy who was disabled and he played the guitar every day. It was an experience.'

Paddy's stay in hospital covered the Christmas period and the nurses wanted to organise something special for their young patients. The children were invited to a party at

James Mackie & Sons Ltd, a Belfast engineering company, four days before Christmas. As an additional treat they were taken to the circus at the Empire Theatre, near Belfast city centre, on Christmas Eve.

A cold January morning saw 1959 dawn and with it the boys' stay in hospital drew to a close. On 4 January they were discharged and sent back to Bangor where a cold winter wind whipped in off Belfast Lough. With his right leg in plaster to strengthen the joint, Paddy had a new set of shoes and a new lease of life. He felt like he had a new set of feet as well; the pain had gone and his steps were less of an effort. He still had the scourge of the callipers to live with but it was a love-hate relationship: he hated his dependency on them but he knew that without them he would not be able to walk. William, on the other hand, was determined that he would get on his feet and walk unaided.

'When you are young you feel you have to get out of the wheelchair. I had this thing with three wheels on it and two crutches under the arm. I could only go certain places in the school. It was a big challenge to me to do away with it. This is where the physiotherapist came in. She came in twice a week. It was through her that I learned to climb stairs. I learned to walk with a crutch at first and then a stick. Then we threw away the stick.'

For William this was his greatest challenge surmounted but fellow boarder Paddy's mind was otherwise occupied. A torrent of emotions ran through his young head, plaguing him with questions about why nobody came to visit him. He knew he wasn't like a lot of the other children who had parents, brothers and sisters to visit them on the weekends or take them out for day trips. He didn't dare ask the nurses why his mum and dad never came to see him. He often sat alone in a corner or out in the grounds playing with the few children who shared his desolation, as parents inside greeted their delighted offspring, who were keen to show off their self-conscious steps.

'I was one of the very few who had nobody. William was there but he had a family. So William's parents visited at the weekends and a lot of other children were like that. I was a very awkward child. I was a very disturbed person. It just annoyed me when other children had their families coming in. I was very angry. I always wondered what happened, why I had nobody. I never conformed to their ways of dealing with things. I was a really bad child, I rebelled against everything. It was a different world. What I hated so much was that there was nobody around me to give me guidance. I got on better with Miss Carson than I did Miss Gilpin. But it was just the environment. William was in a different ball game — he had family. I can't remember anybody in the home that was in the same circumstances as me.'

The hardest times for Paddy were repeatedly sitting through visiting time, watching parents and children being reunited and knowing that no one would be coming for him.

'I was just in the big room and families came in to see the children. I felt very badly left out of it,' he says. 'I saw all the other children and people who were in the home getting visitors. I went into a corner and had a wee cry. I felt bad.

'I do remember some man coming in to see me, but I don't know who he was: a man in his thirties or forties. There was no mention of adoption or anything like that. Whether he just felt sorry for me and just came over to talk to me, I don't know. Nobody ever told me who it was. I was too young at the time to comprehend. But when they all left, we got back together again and, as children will do, played about in the yard.'

Despite the return to fun and games, and the restoration of normality in the home after the visitors had left, Paddy always carried with him a sense of isolation. He was different, even to the children he most related to and identified with. Everybody was not the same; some people had mums and dads. The overwhelming sense of abandonment stirred up feelings of sadness and confusion that turned to rage. He lashed out at the people who were caring for him. He was yearning for the love of a mother and father but his behaviour could not be controlled or tolerated by the staff who had the welfare of twenty-four other children to tend to.

'I got a wee bit of love but not enough, there were that many people in the home. The homes were a lot different to what they are today,' he recalls with discomfort. 'You would never have been shown affection or got a hug or any words of encouragement or praise.'

What separated Paddy even further was the fact that the children in the home had no conception that there were other youngsters without a mother or father. William, who witnessed Paddy's downwardly spiralling behaviour, failed to recognise it at the time as distress.

'I couldn't then but maybe now I can,' he says. 'Most of us had our own people. My parents came down once a week to take me for a drive. Maybe Paddy saw all this. Being kids we weren't aware of people with no parents. We used to give a couple of people lifts home. I didn't know where Paddy went when the school holidays came. The school shut down for two months. There might have been a skeleton staff on. We all went home at the end of June and came back at the end of August.'

William went back to his family home in Newtownabbey, outside Belfast, about a thirty-minute drive from the home. But Paddy spent those long summer holidays with the only family he knew — Stewart Memorial.

'I was never away on holiday from the home. The only time we went away was at Christmas time when a van would call to take us up to Belfast to see the Christmas lights, or Sister Brady from the City Hospital would take us to the Shore Road where the pantomime was on.'

Paddy's emotional state was reflected in his performance at school. His spring term report card recorded his IQ at 86. He had produced below average written work in English and was determined to be a weak reader. In arithmetic, he displayed poor reasoning ability. By the end of the summer term, however, Paddy had settled down and had made a sustained effort throughout the term. There had been a notable improvement in his neatness, spelling and expression in English class. Even in arithmetic he had advanced significantly, getting to grips with weights and measures and handling money. In his handicraft class he was exhibiting more enthusiasm for his work, applying more energy and skill.

One explanation for Paddy's turnaround between the two terms was his newly established membership of the Infantile Paralysis Fellowship. The association was set up to offer support to polio survivors and ensure they did not feel they were forgotten. The polio epidemic seemed finally to be dying out following the discovery of an effective vaccine in 1954. There had been a dramatic fall-off in cases after the north's highest record of infections at 297 in 1957. But there were still survivors living with the repercussions of the vicious disease. The Infantile Paralysis Fellowship was a light in the dark for those survivors. In May 1959 Miss Gilpin wrote to Harold Rankin, Honorary Secretary of the association on the Antrim Road in north Belfast, on behalf of Paddy and a boy called Eugene Scott, expressing their interest in joining:

'The above-named boys, aged 14 years, both victims of poliomyelitis, have expressed a wish to become members of the Infantile Paralysis Association. I am writing to enquire if this could be arranged. It must be confessed that their main object in applying for membership is that they might accompany Robert Graham, a member of your association and a pupil here, when he goes swimming at the baths in Belfast each Saturday evening.'

Mr Rankin had no hesitation in replying that he would be delighted to have the two boys as new members and would even waive the annual fee of two shillings and sixpence. He added that the boys could attend the swimming pool immediately if they wished:

'They are very welcome to come to the baths at once if they wish. If you would be kind enough to ask the gentleman who brings up Robert Graham to also bring these two boys, I am sure he would do so. When contacting the driver, you could mention my name, and I am sure he would be willing to carry out this duty.'

Paddy was to begin a new and enduring relationship with Mr Rankin, which would see him through the next ten years. His outings to the Ormeau Baths in Belfast were adventures he awaited with impatient zeal each Saturday. The Fellowship opened a whole new world for him. He took off into the city for a few hours of fun and was treated with affection and respect by Mr Rankin and the older members of the association. Over the course of that summer in 1959, as well as attending the pool, Paddy was invited on car runs and the Fellowship's annual coach tour. The staff noticed a very welcome change in Paddy and were keen to encourage it. Miss Gilpin had established a good relationship with the association and placed her full trust in Mr Rankin when it came to taking care of her boys. All was peaceful in Paddy's world and, thus, also in the world of Stewart Memorial. Despite what he perceived as its shortcomings, this was the place that held Paddy's first memories, where he took his first steps, where he first knew both happiness and pain. He had grown to love the kindly nurses who had encouraging words for him and whose coveted time he had to himself during the summer months. He disliked, as children do, domineering and authoritarian figures in the form of the head matron, Miss Gilpin, and the home manager, Jim Dornan. In his short life he had grabbed what attention he could by whatever means he could, finding that creating circumstances in which he became the centre of attention — for good or bad — was the only way to feel loved. Paddy survived on these scraps of affection like the proverbial dog anxiously waiting for crumbs to fall from the proverbial dinner table. But when his behaviour became too much to handle Paddy would once again pay the price for being abandoned.

2

THE END OF the summer of 1959 brought with it a sharp smack of reality to the staff of Stewart Memorial. The more placid side to Paddy, which they had recently witnessed, began to fall by the wayside in August. The insolent and headstrong Paddy of old was swiftly returning and his behaviour was once again a cause of disruption in the home.

Paddy had become obsessed with outside activities, especially the outings with Mr Rankin and the Infantile Paralysis Fellowship. In his mind if he was invited to go somewhere then it was his right to go. Approaching fifteen years of age, he was too old and too big for detention in the toy box, and the occasional smack across the backside only briefly dispelled his tantrums. So Miss Gilpin resorted to withdrawing one of Paddy's treasured retreats as punishment for his disobedience. He had been given permission to attend a car run organised by Mountainview Social Club for the Fellowship in mid-August. Four days before the outing that consent was withdrawn. Miss Gilpin wrote to Mr Rankin to inform him that 'due to a change of plans' Paddy would not be attending. To Miss Gilpin's mind Paddy was becoming a little too accustomed to setting off into the city to the swimming baths, and for jaunts here and there. His fifteenth birthday was only a month off and, as far as he was concerned, he should be allowed to do what he wanted. Miss Gilpin, however, was determined to do all in her power to instil some obedience in him.

Initially, banning him from the Fellowship's outing appeared to have the desired effect.

As expected, he did not take his punishment well but the threat of missing future trips scared him into submission. He stormed about the home, making his displeasure known to all who strayed across his path but, nonetheless, he endured his penance. A bigger storm was brewing. September was approaching and with it a new year in the Boys' Brigade. Paddy knew he would have to behave if he was to start back with the rest of his friends. Earlier in the year he had earned his three-year service badge and he was determined that this year he would impress the brigade leader, Hugh Brown, by adding another badge to his jacket.

Stewart Memorial had longstanding ties with the Boys' Brigade, running back to 1912, when the brigade started an annual collection for the institute's upkeep. Paddy's membership was greatly encouraged by the school principal, not only as a way to keep him out of mischief, but also to teach him some valuable skills and principles. To Paddy the brigade was a chance to break free from the home for a few hours and escape the constant watch of his 'warders'. These periods of freedom were enhanced by the great improvement in his walking.

Callipers were, as ever, a permanent fixture in his life. On his left leg he carried a double iron support calliper which allowed him to bend at the knee. A small cork had been added to the base of his left shoe to even out his posture, and his feet and toes had consistently improved. The doctors noted that he was walking well despite his tendency to carry all his weight on his right foot. Weighing in at seven stone, four-and-a-half pounds, his weight was not substantial for a teenager of his age, but because he hitched up his shoulders and pressed his weight onto his right foot, it was enough to create problems for his spine. The doctors, however, were satisfied that, with regular stretching and posture exercises, his mobility would continue to improve. It was good news for Paddy and confirmed to him that he was ready to fly solo.

September came and went and Paddy returned to the Boys' Brigade. Firmly ensconced in the brigade's ranks he threw himself into his duties. By now growing increasingly weary of being told what to do and living by the home's rules, he decided that he was going to live by his own rules from now on. The storm that had been brewing was coming to a head. On Saturday, 21 November, it broke. That morning Paddy informed Miss Gilpin he was going out to deliver envelopes for Boys' Brigade Week. He told her he would not be back in time for dinner at 12.30pm. Miss Gilpin insisted that Paddy return at the usual time and continue his canvassing later in the afternoon.

'He set off in a truculent mood,' her report of that day recorded.

Disobeying Miss Gilpin's wishes Paddy returned at 2.30pm 'in a defiant frame of mind'.

Miss Gilpin had kept Paddy's dinner but he refused to eat it. After discussing his behaviour with the matron, Miss Gilpin decided to punish him for his 'defiance and disobedience' by forbidding him to go to swimming at the Ormeau Baths that evening. Later, Paddy could not be found in the home. Miss Gilpin presumed he had gone to the Boys' Brigade Club in Bangor. At 9.30pm Mrs Herron from Palestine Street in Belfast telephoned the home to tell Miss Gilpin that Paddy had arrived at her home and was refusing to return to Bangor. Paddy had spent several weekends with Mrs Herron and her husband Victor, who had a son who had survived polio. Mrs Herron's husband was not home that evening and she found Paddy extremely difficult to cope with on her own. Miss Gilpin contacted the home's manager, Mr Dornan, and explained the situation to him. He instructed her to phone the police at the barracks in Donegall Pass in Belfast. The police agreed to collect Paddy and keep him at the barracks until Mr Dornan arrived. When Paddy was escorted back to the home by Mr Dornan at 11.30pm, he exploded into an uncontrollable rage.

'He was extremely violent, rude and threatening,' Miss Gilpin reported. 'He tried to strike Mr Dornan and used most insulting and filthy language. He yelled and rushed about like a madman, kicking articles across the dormitory. He refused to go to bed.'

One too many reprimands had pushed Paddy over the edge and he'd lost it. All his pent-up anger was unleashed and Mr Dornan's jaw was in the wrong place at the wrong time.

'I went berserk and I just banged him. I hit him across the face,' he says.

Paddy spits out these words with vitriol as he recollects the incident in Stewart Memorial. He immediately jumps to the defence of his teenage self, forced to take matters literally into his own hands.

'I was chastised very badly, getting locked in too many cupboards. I threw the head up. It's understandable when you are young like that. It was terrible altogether.'

Unable to reason with Paddy or restrain him, the matron, Mr Dornan and Miss Gilpin left him in the dormitory. Miss Gilpin and the matron stayed up until 1am and then the lights were turned out and all was quiet. But punching Mr Dornan was the last straw for Miss Gilpin. She had been used to Paddy's 'violent, emotional outbursts' but she had never seen him in such a mad rage.

'He appeared to be on the verge of almost insanity' was how she concluded her report.

Paddy was so caught up in his rage that night he failed to register that, by punching Mr Dornan, he had effectively sounded the death knell for his time in Stewart Memorial.

In the eyes of the home management there was only one solution — to move the problem elsewhere. The nurses were not trained to deal with restless children with a tendency for violence. The severity of Paddy's offence demanded that he be removed from the home. Who knew what he would do next? They could not and would not risk any further fits of fury. Miss Gilpin immediately informed Dr Walby at the Belfast Education Authority of the episode. He arranged with Mr Green at Down Welfare to have Paddy interviewed with a view to his removal to another institution.

'The next thing I knew I was on my way,' Paddy recalls.

On the cold winter Monday morning of 23 November 1959, just two days after his riotous behaviour, Paddy was removed from Stewart Memorial and bundled off to St Leonard's home in Warrenpoint, County Down, more than forty-five miles from Bangor. His sojourn there was to be little over a month long, but the swiftness with which his stay in Stewart Memorial was cut short left an indelible imprint on his mind. In the same way that he'd been ripped from the safety of his mother's arms as an infant, Paddy was now torn from the only place he'd ever known as home. This time, however, he was old enough to remember the pain of separation and rejection. During the car journey from Bangor to Warrenpoint, Paddy's body was numbed with fear but his mind was racing with thoughts about where he was going and what they were going to do with him once he got there. He knew he had done a bad thing by punching Mr Dornan but he was sorry and he would tell them that if they would just take him back to the home. He felt like a faulty product being removed from the production line and tossed aside for a malfunction beyond his control.

Paddy maintains they didn't understand what it was like for him: all those years of toeing the line, going along with their rules, their prayers, their ways. He had just snapped. But when he did, he crossed the line and, just like that, he became an outsider, alien to them. He was on the other side from those he had most identified with. How quickly they had rejected him. He was banished from their controlled little world with Gospel meetings and toy chests. But all the memories, all the experiences he had ever had, started and ended there. If they didn't want him, who would?

'When I left Stewart Memorial to go to St Leonard's my suitcase was packed and that was that. I had no idea where I was going. Although there was no affection, the Stewart Memorial was the only place I'd known as home. The only person I was really friendly with was William and he was just left behind.'

While Paddy can't remember being physically removed from Stewart Memorial, he has very lucid memories of being deposited at St Leonard's, scared and alone.

'My memory is of landing on the doorstep. It was a big house with a long avenue set back from the road; a big, yellow building. I didn't feel great to be there. It was a totally different environment. I missed my mates. I missed William.'

Paddy admits it was his blatantly disruptive behaviour that forced his removal from Stewart Memorial but this knowledge didn't stop the questions plaguing him as to why he was offloaded to the home in Warrenpoint. He was miles away from the familiar surroundings of the Bangor coast and his friends. It was quite a shock to leave a place where he was one of the oldest residents and arrive at another where he was by far the youngest. Paddy had been placed in a home for the elderly.

'I was sent to St Leonard's because I was too much to handle, because I was so unruly. But what got me was me at my age, with all the old people. I remember asking myself why I had been put in there. Because they had nowhere else to put me? Because I was so disruptive to the other children in the home in Bangor? I didn't know how long I was going to be there.'

While Paddy was disoriented at being uprooted from Stewart Memorial he was, at the same time, glad to have escaped what he viewed as its oppressive regime and his constant feeling of displacement. He had shared a common bond with the children through his disability but he always felt distinct from them because he had no parents and no family; no allowances had been made for this. He was treated just like the rest of the children who had mummies and daddies who came to visit them, delighted to see the progress their 'imperfect little children' were making. The vacuum created by the lack of familial love and warmth frustrated him and led to him 'acting out'. But his skirmishes were met with unfeeling discipline and religion; the message was clear: 'conform or be punished'. There was little time for emotions or tantrums in the business of growing up. It was this which Paddy could not handle. It was a constant heartache to witness children with families being cuddled and held in warm embraces by their loving parents. He had to look on longingly, knowing that he wouldn't be on the receiving end of any hugs or kisses, always hopeful that one day his parents would turn up and claim him. However, they never came and, instead, he learned to fade into the background. The only thing he could do to steal a little attention for himself was to create havoc but then he was only reprimanded and ostracised. Over the years this anger burrowed away inside him and, reinforced by other frustrations, consumed him with rancour. He feels that his extradition from Stewart Memorial helped free him from his plight.

'I was dumbfounded but in a way too I was glad to get out of the home in Bangor. It was sort of an escape because of all the years in it, the torment,' Paddy says, quickly adding 'the running of it'.

'At least with St Leonard's there were older people, but I wasn't treated too badly. I got on all right with the old people. I always found that Warrenpoint was a nice part of the world. The nurses took me out on walks down to the seaside. They weren't bad, they looked after me, they didn't hit me or anything there,' he recalls.

There was no schooling in the home and Paddy was very

much left to his own devices: pottering about, whiling away the hours and, most importantly, keeping out of mischief.

It was a relief not to have to trek out to Gospel meetings as he had to do in Stewart Memorial, but this annoyance would have at least brought some variety to his days and alleviated the boredom of his alert young mind. Instead, Paddy spent idle hours preoccupied with thoughts of his friends back in Bangor, wondering if they thought about him, and mulling over how long this punishment would last.

'I don't know what I did all day. I can't remember going to school. I had no company.

'I just mixed in with the old people because I wasn't let out on my own. I know I never went to church while I was there. It wasn't so much a Gospel home like Stewart Memorial. It was of mixed religion — but I wouldn't have paid much attention to that, it never dawned on me.

'In the home in Bangor I had a few mates, but in St Leonard's I had no friends. It was just the routine: getting up in the morning, getting my breakfast, hanging about, no work to do — just boredom in general. At the table where I ate there was a man I'll remember till the day I die; he was in a wheelchair and he only had one leg and he would talk to me, about what, I don't know. There were about twenty of us. I didn't have many dealings with the staff, they were too busy.'

St Leonard's was, in fact, the antithesis of Stewart Memorial. There was no Gospel to learn, no meetings to traipse to, no regimented chores to do, no toy boxes to be locked in, no friends to lark about with, and no regime to fight against. By sending him to this place they had achieved their aim and taken the wind out of his sails; but what had they left him with? He was drifting aimlessly in no direction. Still these frustrations burned inside him, fuelling him to do something. He needed something to fight for but they had taken all. True, he blended seamlessly into the background as the staff went about their business but, where previously this would have led him to act out to attract their attention, now he just wanted to be free from the monotony of it all. He felt himself stagnating, deprived of stimuli in the form of school or friends, all of this pent-up energy surging around inside him. He wanted to be free of St Leonard's and the old people who seemed to have accepted their lot and were passively trudging through each day. They were harmless and he had grown fond of some of them but he was a spirited fifteen-year-old with raging hormones and unpredictable emotions. He shuddered at the thought of having to stay there and become like them, sedentary and resigned to their fate. It wasn't long before this horror deluged his mind and his fight-or-flight response kicked in. Hardly surprising then that, during the course of Paddy's month-long stay at St Leonard's, the prospect of escape sprang to mind.

'I seemed to be the only young person there. That's probably why I ran away so much, wondering, "What am I doing here? Why did they put me in here?"'

His few bids for freedom were thwarted every time by the police, who were always two steps ahead of him, forewarned by staff at the home that Paddy was on the run again.

'In those days I was seven-and-a-half stone, I was young, healthy and reasonably fit. I was always running down the avenue with my two callipers on, and every time the police were waiting at the bottom to bring me back again,' he says, laughing at the memory.

To the police the sight of a disabled teen making an earnest bolt for freedom, weighed down by heavy metal callipers, must have stirred a mixture of admiration, amusement and pity. But for Paddy, for a few brief moments, as he was stealing away from the confines of the home, he was almost within reach of that elusive liberty. He didn't know where he was running to; he just knew he wanted to be free.

'I just wanted to get away. It was maybe just badness. I couldn't run fast — but I could run.'

Run though he might, he was soon scooped up by the constabulary, bundled into the car, and returned safely to the home where there was no reprimand, only shaking heads and disappointment.

'The police laughed at me and took me back up in the car. I was crying. I was more scared of the police in those days. Seeing a big man in uniform was a scary sight. I was a bit timid then.'

3

FREEDOM EVENTUALLY DID beckon for Paddy and shortly after his last few escape bids his prayers were answered when he was released from St Leonard's care. As he was ushered out of the home, a new decade was ushered in. On 8 January 1960 he was deposited in a car and whisked away from the picturesque shores of Warrenpoint to the big city lights of Belfast. At sixteen Paddy was expected to be able to handle himself but he was at a disadvantage from the start. Having spent the previous month in a home with elderly, disabled people and, having had little interaction with other teenagers, he found himself in a hostel for young men. The headstrong, calliper-laden teen, who had successfully wreaked havoc in both his previous homes, now found himself thrown into the ring with teenagers for whom violence was a mode for survival and a way of life. For all the years he had spent practising the art of mischief to attract attention, he was now to put comparable, if not more, effort into staying both out of trouble and out of sight.

The home Paddy was sent to on that January morning was the Belfast Welfare Hostel at 236 Newtownards Road, otherwise known as Kincora.

Paddy was unaware of the scandal that was to unfurl about the very home whose doors he had just walked through. It would be two decades before the horrific details of sexual abuse at the hands of carers in Kincora's employment would fill papers across the country, begging answers of the social services and the police. The very mention of Kincora has become synonymous with that scandal, unearthed there by the *Irish Independent* newspaper in 1980 — the worst case of its kind at the time. The home, in the east of the city, was a publicly-run hostel set up in 1959 to provide accommodation and care for young people. But, as the newspaper would reveal, children at the home were subjected to sexual abuse from 1960 to 1980. In December 1981 five men, including William McGrath, the former housemaster of Kincora, and his two colleagues, Joe Mains, a former warden at the home, and Raymond Semple, a deputy warden, were jailed. The three men pleaded guilty to twenty-eight charges of sexual offences against boys in their care. The day after the trial ended, another newspaper, the *Irish Times*, revealed that a British army intelligence officer had informed journalists in 1975 that McGrath was a homosexual — a crime in Northern Ireland until 1982 — and a member of the violent extreme loyalist paramilitary group, Tara.

Allegations of a cover-up were rife. In the political aftermath, amidst a constant barrage of calls for a public inquiry, Ian Paisley, leader of the Democratic Unionist Party, denied having any knowledge of the scandal before it became public. He subsequently admitted, in January 1982, that he had been given evidence in 1975 that McGrath was a homosexual, although he insisted he did not know that McGrath was working in Kincora.

There was an eruption of media claims that the police force of the time, the Royal Ulster Constabulary (RUC), had known about the abuse in 1976 but authorities had blocked an investigation into an alleged homosexual prostitution ring involving British officials in the Northern Ireland Office (NIO), policemen, legal figures and boys in care at Kincora and other homes run by the Eastern Health Board. Suggestions also arose that the alleged cover-up was designed to blackmail prominent members of loyalist paramilitary groups into becoming informers. As a known member of Tara, there were claims that McGrath was working for the British military intelligence group, MI5, and that the security forces had ignored the plight of boys at Kincora to safeguard their informant. In 1983 the findings of an inquiry into the RUC's handling of the Kincora scandal found no evidence to substantiate claims of a vice ring allegedly run from the home. However, in 1985, the *Irish Times* turned up a British army document which contradicted British government assurances that there was no cover-up. The RUC reopened its investigation into Kincora following the appearance of the document which claimed that the police, the army and the NIO were all aware of sexual assaults on Kincora residents as far back as 1974. The army document was signed by Colin Wallace, a senior British army information officer at the time.

Wallace had been working for the army's information policy unit, a black propaganda and psychological warfare agency attached to the press desk at the army's Northern Ireland headquarters in Lisburn. He claimed he had been involved in a 'dirty tricks' campaign which was designed to discredit republican and loyalist paramilitary groups and later leading politicians. In 1990 there were renewed calls for a government explanation of the Kincora scandal after Wallace told the press that he had been given conflicting instructions from the army and MI5 in the early 1970s on what to do with information about the abuse. Wallace claimed the army told him to release the details about Kincora to the media and that, conversely, MI5 had instructed him to use Kincora to discredit political leaders in the north. Since 1980 there have been six inquiries into the depraved activities at Kincora but none has exposed how deep the scandal ran, nor have they served to satisfy the public outcry as to how the abuse was allowed to continue for so long.

Mercifully for Paddy, while he was beaten, he was spared the ordeal of sexual abuse during his stay in Kincora, and was oblivious to the molestation taking place there.

The revelations in 1980 were as much a surprise to him as they were to the rest of Northern Ireland. Joining the home shortly after its opening, Paddy lived with the boys who were to face abuse at the hands of pederasts Mains, McGrath and Semple. Paddy disliked Mains from the outset and says the feeling was mutual, although he does recall that the warden had his 'wee favourites'.

'At the start it was all right, I toed the line and got on fine. Boys kept coming and going in the home — they didn't stay long,' he says. 'Mains was a big, tough-looking man who smoked a pipe. He was very authoritative. He hated my guts. I just did not get on with the man at all. I used to have run-ins with him and he would put me to bed early or clip me round the ear. There were guys that were his "lick boys";

they would tell him when I had exchanged bus tokens for cigarettes. They touted on me.'

Paddy would have been given bus tokens instead of a bus fare by Mains at the start of every week to take him to work and back, but he would often hold on to a few of the tokens and swap them for cigarettes with one of the bus conductors he was friendly with.

He had no inkling that there was anything untoward happening behind the closed doors in the home but, looking back, Paddy says there were a few things he thought were odd at the time.

'I knew nothing about the abuse. The only thing I recollect was that me and the other boys used to wonder what they were doing in the office. We just thought they were in there having a drink or a smoke. I never dreamt there was anything untoward happening. We were next door in the TV room. The only time I was in his office was to get bus tokens or to be reprimanded.'

Paddy does not recall ever being under Raymond Semple's care but he does remember that Semple, who was appointed as a deputy warden in 1964, was a regular visitor to Kincora. Paddy presumed that Semple was just Mains' friend and had no idea that the men were taking advantage of vulnerable boys as young as twelve.

'Semple came in every Sunday night and, as far as I understood, he was Mains' mate and they were just socialising,' he remembers. 'Every Sunday night it seemed to happen, another big mate of his would come down from Dundonald (on the eastern outskirts of Belfast) but there were only about three boys who went into his office. When I say boys, they were about twelve, thirteen or fourteen.'

Revelations of the sex abuse in Kincora came as a shock

to Paddy. He escaped unscathed and, for once in his life, he was grateful for his disability, believing it to have been a deterrent to Mains.

'I was never sexually abused or anything like that. I didn't hear about the scandal until I was out working and I happened to be listening to the news and I thought, "God, is that the same place I was in?" When I thought about it, I wondered what else could have been going on in there apart from drinking and smoking.

'It was one of the few times that I was glad that I had polio. I wasn't attractive enough or whatever, although having said that I wouldn't have stood for it because I could look after myself in those days. I was the only person with a disability in Kincora and I had the odd wee skirmish,' he admits with a mischievous smile.

But, despite this new-found confidence, Paddy loathed every minute in Kincora. He had spent his entire life in care in controlled environments where things were, at least on the surface, done by the book. There was no room for manoeuvre, it was suffocating and oppressing — rules, routine and retribution. Strangely, despite, or perhaps because of, the clandestine goings-on in Kincora, Paddy felt it was one of the most stifling of homes he had lived in. A tight rein was kept on all the boys who were instructed to return to the home immediately after school or work. Failure to adhere to the rules would not be taken lightly.

'You didn't go out in Kincora. Once you came in from work that was it, you were in for the night. I hated it. I hated every minute of it. I couldn't get out of it quick enough. I hated the environment, the whole system. It was all welfare, welfare. By that stage I had been in so many homes I didn't know whether I was coming or going. It was mind-melting. When I left there I was delighted.'

While at Kincora Paddy briefly attended Park Parade Secondary School, which was opposite Ormeau Park, on the corner of the Ormeau Embankment where it meets the Ravenhill Road. He didn't have much time for education and, after dispensing with school, he couldn't wait to start earning his own money. Practically uneducated, there wasn't much in the line of work for Paddy aside from unskilled manual labour jobs. His first job was in Devonshire Laundry on the Ravenhill Road in the south of the city. Hot, sweaty and dank, it was back-breaking work and not a job he derived any pleasure from, but it brought in the cash and was his first step on the ladder to independence and self-sufficiency.

'It was very heavy work, pushing buggies filled with wet sheets along the tracks. I hated it, it was bloody hard work.'

Taking his leave from the laundry, Paddy did some odd shifts for the Sunblest Bakery at Bloomfield Avenue in east Belfast. Despite the early morning starts he preferred it to his job in the laundry.

'I worked for Sunblest, the bread people. The man used to rap me up in the mornings with the big pole they used for pulling out their trays from the back of the van. I was his helper for an extra couple of shillings. I started at 5.30am and didn't finish until 12pm or 1pm. He was a nice man from the Ravenhill Road.'

Paddy had quite an array of jobs while in Kincora but the one he found the most interesting and intense was at the Moygashel group's factory on the Donegall Road, where he made uniforms for the United States Air Force. He travelled to work in style, in the sidecar of a motorbike. He felt he was quite the sight first thing in the morning, strapping his helmet tightly on, throwing his legs awkwardly over the door and whizzing into work.

'This guy used to give me a lift from Kincora in his sidecar. One day I decided to sit on the back of the bike and I fell off,' Paddy says, roaring with laughter. 'I was alright but I learned my lesson after that and stuck to the sidecar.'

Once safely at work there was the odd splash of variety cast into the day in the shape of dazzling white fabric. In complete contrast to the usual coarse army material the workers fashioned into soldiers' uniforms, reams of white cloth were occasionally thrown across sewing machines for machinists to transform into tuxedos for American officers they would never see sporting the fruits of their labour. With not an officer or a gentleman in sight, Paddy and his two hundred-odd colleagues worked hard for their pay.

'We made the waistcoats and the trousers to go with the tuxedos — they were a strange sight. It was a nightmare of a place sometimes.'

It was not only the size of the factory that made it a nightmare for Paddy. He was singled out by his fellow workers because of his disability and given a nickname which cut him to the bone. The tougher Belfast men, who didn't give a damn how hard it was for Paddy to get about, had no time to spare for his feelings: he was fair game. They were just having a laugh and, more often than not, it was he who was the butt of their jokes.

'I was always called Joe Grimshaw. "Here comes wee Joe," they would say. Some of them were very cruel; because of my disability they would shout up the factory floor, "Here comes half-pint Joe." I hated that,' he says, visibly recoiling at the memory.

Aside from the bullies, there were a few mischievous older women who liked to wind him up. Although they were having fun at his expense, he was at least in on their jokes and he took it all in good spirit. Often, when he was midway through making a pair of trousers, they would tamper with his sewing machine.

'The wee old women would cut the thread on the machine when I was putting the inside pockets into the trousers. It was just for devilment,' he laughs. 'I was a bit annoyed at the same time because you had a certain amount to get through in a day to get your pay.'

Paddy spent a brief spell in a similar line of work with T J Magee Ltd in Royal Avenue in the city centre. Magee's made Irish 'Thornproof suits', as an advert from the time reads, 'in short, medium and long fittings in each chest size. Also made to measure.'

Paddy learned a lot about the 'made to measure' trade while at Magee's but one particular area of expertise he picked up stands out in his mind.

'Magee's was good craic. Upstairs there was a sewing room where they made the suits. You got two or three fittings in those days — it was right expensive to get a suit made. That was some experience. There were these two guys who worked there: one was deaf and the other was dumb and they were always good craic. They were absolutely fantastic, they showed me everything, how to sew, the whole lot. But my first job in the mornings was to feed the pigeons out the window. The noise of them would have put you batty. I hated that and I still hate pigeons to this day.'

Away from work, Paddy was a regular at the Northern Ireland Polio Fellowship meetings, an organisation created to provide practical support to polio survivors. It was through the Fellowship that he met another polio survivor, Eddie McCrory. The two came across each other in 1960 through the Fellowship Swimming Club and, although Eddie was only eight and Paddy nearly sixteen, the two became firm friends. Paddy had been going to the Polio Fellowship's outings to the Ormeau Baths since 1959 while he was still in Stewart Memorial. The Fellowship met up every Saturday night for the swimming club which was a great way for polio survivors to make new friends and keep in touch with old ones. With his larger than life personality, Paddy wasn't someone who faded into the background. Over the years he had earned a reputation for larking around. So when he nearly drowned one night during a swimming session, it was some time before anyone cottoned on that he was in trouble and wasn't just acting the eejit. Eddie remembers watching in disbelief as Paddy plummeted towards the bottom of the pool.

'We used to have a gala every year for the Polio Fellowship. Well, this night, Paddy had had a big fry before he went into the water and halfway up the length, he took cramp and just went down. We were all just looking, saying, "Is he messing or something?" We thought he was acting the wag. But then somebody dived in and saved him.'

Paddy sheepishly recalls that it was a woman called Shirley Foster, from Belfast's Donegall Road, who came to his rescue.

'Big Shirley, she was the swimming instructor, and she pulled me up but that put paid to my swimming for a while,' he remembers.

Aside from the occasional dramas sparked by Paddy's antics, Eddie said there was always a great atmosphere at the swimming baths. He recalls that his sister Teresa, who was the same age as Paddy, was a regular spectator at the gala events. He also vaguely recalls Teresa wheeling him up to visit Paddy in Kincora one Sunday afternoon. The two lads may not have realised at the time but Teresa had her own reasons for volunteering to bring Eddie up to visit Paddy. She had taken a shine to Paddy and, as the boys chatted, it gave her a chance to have a flirt with him. It would soon transpire that Paddy felt the same.

Paddy had no shortage of jobs while staying at Kincora. One was a position in Cregagh Dairies, which he got through a contact with the Polio Fellowship.

'People called the Smith Brothers owned it. One of the brothers was a trustee of the Polio Fellowship,' he says. 'There were about ten of us working together. I used to cut the wellies half way up my calf so that they would fit over my boots. We had to wear white coats and hats. Only about three men worked in it with me and they were old hands who had worked there for years. There were women too and there was one elderly lady and she was some laugh.'

Paddy was now older, a little wiser and felt surer on his feet than ever. He loved working in the dairy factory, watching the huge churns mixing and folding their golden mixture into butter. But when Paddy slipped up, he slipped up in style and it was one such slip that saw him landing up to his neck in it.

'I was always hosing things down and the floor was always wet and very slippery. This day, I must have been rushing to do something and I slipped and went head-first into one of the big butter churns. I threw my hands out in front of me and just went head-first into the butter. The churn was about ten feet deep. It wasn't going around or anything but it was full of cream. They hoisted me out and just went on making the butter. I was just sorry it wasn't Bushmills: I would have gone under fourteen times before they would have got me out.'

Willy Wonka's Chocolate Factory it certainly was not and when Paddy was scrubbed up it was straight back to his cleaning duties with a healthy dose of 'slagging' from his fellow workers.

'This elderly lady, when she saw me going into the butter she couldn't stop laughing. She was in a complete wrinkle.'

4

FROM THE LEAFY suburbia of east Belfast surrounding Kincora Boys' Home, Paddy was moved, again with no explanation, to the Boys' Residential Home in the suburbs of south Belfast. It was 1961 and seventeen-year-old Paddy was eager to leave care. The news that this would be his last home could not have been more welcome. The home on Blacks Road, running between the Stewartstown Road in west Belfast and the Upper Lisburn Road in south Belfast, was managed by the Reverend Gilmore and his wife. It came under the auspices of the Presbyterian Church in Ireland but was the brainchild of the Reverend William John Thompson, who had long been of service to young men left stranded by circumstances beyond their control. Reverend Thompson started his work in the 1930s by setting up clubs for unemployed men, young boys and girls and, in 1943, he persuaded the church's general assembly to open a residence for homeless boys and those from the country who had come to the city to serve their apprenticeships.

Situated in a predominantly affluent Protestant area, the home was ideally situated to keep some of its more wayward residents on the straight and narrow.

'The boys were in trouble with the law,' says Paddy. 'There were only about twelve people in it, four in every room. It was an entirely different environment. It was all male and they were in their late teens. I was among the youngest.'

Paddy was by now very used to living with other teenagers but he found some of the new home's residents a little on the wild side. He spent a lot of his time in a constant state of fear. Barely five foot, four inches and seven-and-a-half stone in weight, he was a mere shadow to the rougher boys whom he found terrifying in stature, and menacing in personality.

'I was the only disabled person in the place and I was scared a lot of the time, very much so. I was scared they would hurt me, scared they'd do something bad to me. It was a rough home. You felt intimidated all the time. The boys were older than me. They were Belfast street boys: they came through the ranks; they knew how to look after themselves but to me it was a culture shock.'

Paddy stood staring out the window to the ground below where his callipers, boots and bed lay strewn. It was his first night in a new home. Some welcome this was — home, what did that mean anyway? This wasn't his home, just like Kincora hadn't been, or St Leonard's before that. The only home he had ever known was the one he had been turfed out of, and since then he had been skimming across the surface of other places that 'they' — those in charge — had decided would serve as his 'home' for as short or long as they wished. He had learned not to get attached to anyone, anywhere or anything. He didn't dare. There seemed to be no logic or warning to his removal from each dwelling. He wouldn't satisfy them by getting upset — not that he cared for any of those places anyway. And they had got it wrong again. Here, he was like an odd sock, sticking out among the rest of the boys who seemed to feel like they belonged there. They either pretended not to notice him or taunted him. What had he done to deserve a life like this? Wasn't it enough that he had no family; that he had had to live since childhood with the disabilities accrued through polio? But now, the bullies would not even give him the space to live unfettered. In the past his fellow inmates had been his allies, united in their aversion to authority. But in this dark, new world his would-be allies had turned on him — he was an object of fun to be ridiculed and tormented.

A sharp taste of disgust rose in his throat, one which he had tasted many times before and, many times, forced back down. He wanted his family to come and claim him. He was ready to go. He had always been ready, patiently waiting. He was sorry for whatever it was that he had done to make them abandon him. He just wanted to go home. There was no anger housed here, just an overpowering sense of vulnerability without them. He wanted to have a mum, a dad, brothers and sisters and then let the world know: 'Enough is enough, I have a family too; so now you can butt out and leave me alone.' All he wanted was to be left alone to make his own way. It was a hard enough road to walk without the obstacles these bullies put in his way.

'I went up to my room after I arrived and my bed was out on the lawn. They had thrown it, my callipers and my boots out the window,' Paddy recalls with a feigned humour that quickly fades into a weak smile. 'You daren't have gone to the staff and told them what was happening, it really wasn't done.'

'Touting' was not permissible unless he wanted to bring a world of hassle crashing down upon him. All he could do was accept that he was lost in a system in which there seemed to be no justice for the unwanted and unloved. In an unfamiliar city he had nowhere to run to this time. Being a child of the system, or a 'wee abandoned', as Paddy calls himself, he could not break free from the restraints of an organisation which laid claim to him. Discarded at birth he had become property of the state. Within a family, Paddy reasoned, he could at least have taken his leave and they would have let him go his own way until those transparent familial bonds pulled him back to them, where they could keep an eye on him until they were ready, at last, to indulge his independence.

But a child of the system seldom has that luxury. They are forever a part of that network of rules and obligations, locked in an unfeeling embrace determined to restrain them until the umbilical cord is brutally, and without warning, severed.

Unfortunately for Paddy the fears he felt on his introduction to his new surroundings were well-founded. The home was a charged place where trouble was liable to break out at any moment and more often than not it did, despite the best efforts of those in charge to dissolve it. A violent scuffle Paddy witnessed at dinner one night left him emotionally scarred for the duration of his stay at the Boys' Residential Home.

'We were in the room where we got our meals served and we were queuing at the hatch. An argument started and I saw one fella sticking a penknife into the other one's side.

The Reverend Gilmore arrived and they got the fella sorted out — he wasn't badly hurt. But when I went up to the dormitories the boy who did it said to me, "You didn't see that." It had a traumatic effect on me. It was a home I was very scared in all the time. I couldn't handle myself because of my disability.'

Paddy's vulnerability was obvious to all who looked at him. Small and slight, he had a handicap that distinguished him from everyone else. To Paddy his callipers were an annoyance that had become a way of life but to others they made him distinctive and alien and, therefore, a target.

The rough teenagers, like a pack of wolves, picked the awkward teen off like a defenceless animal, and there was little he could do to protect himself from the onslaught.

He was trapped. His fear collapsed in around him and wrapped itself like a blanket about his body. Paddy prepared to spend the rest of his time in the home under a wave of interminable distress. That was until he met Mervyn McWilliams.

'It was Big Mervyn who helped me. He looked after me and taught me the ways of the world. He was able to look after himself. I saw him fighting a couple of times and sorting them out. He was in the home when I arrived there. We got on like a house on fire. I never really got on with any of the rest of them. He taught me to look after myself. But I still shied away from trouble.'

Like the big brother Paddy had never had, Mervyn stepped in to shield him from the rowdy lads. An imposing character, eighteen-year-old Mervyn, originally from Lisburn, had no problem in looking after himself. A year older than Paddy, he was a 'big tall chap' and more streetwise than the timid newcomer. Unlike a lot of the teenagers in the Boys' Residential Home, Mervyn had not been in trouble with the law. His mother had remarried following his father's death when Mervyn was fifteen. He and his stepfather did not see eye to eye so he felt he had no choice but to leave his mother in her new marriage without him. The Boys' Residential Home was his safe haven. Coming from an unhappy home Mervyn felt for Paddy whom he knew had no family and was a prime target for the tougher Belfast boys.

'He was a quiet wee fella,' says Mervyn. 'I had a funny feeling that he was orphaned, just thrown to the side. There were a few roughs about there — they had a choice of prison or the home, so they took the home. They were a wee bit hard on Paddy, so I just got them settled down. They were taking his calliper at night and throwing it out the bedroom window. Then I got it stopped to give him a bit of peace. I just told them that if they didn't leave him alone then I would deal with them.'

Sufficiently scared, the boys backed off and left Paddy alone. Despite the odd scuffle, Mervyn claims to have enjoyed his time in care. The ministers responsible for taking care of the boys took a great interest in their welfare and did all in their power to make it feel like a real home, which was a godsend for Mervyn.

'The Reverend W J Thompson was a fundraiser for the home. He came once a week to chat to the boys and see how they were getting on. Reverend Gilmore and his wife were residents and there was another young couple, he was a groundsman and she did cooking. We were terribly well fed and well looked after.'

In Mervyn's eyes the home was one of the best things that could have happened to him and the other boys under its supervision. Staying in his mother's house with his stepfather was not an option and the home was a relaxed environment with even-handed discipline that Mervyn could handle just fine.

'It did no harm at all. If anything, it did a lot of them some good — gave them a bit of sense. A couple absconded but they got them and brought them back again and they wised up.'

Despite Meryvn's interventions and brotherly advice, the stabbing in the canteen had done its damage for Paddy. He found it hard to relax his guard under the unremitting threat of violence. The hardness of the home had eaten away at his already waning and fragile mental state, and he lapsed into a mild depression. They were dark days for Paddy. He didn't walk the same as the other lads; had he, they might have found him less of a figure of fun and ridicule. So finding the middle ground between fight or flight, he half-heartedly employed the ducking and diving tactics Meryvn had urged him to use to keep out of the rough boys' way. He was resigned to his misery but Meryvn was not content to let things lie. He gave as good as he got and continued to watch Paddy's back, weighing in whenever it was necessary. He knew he wasn't always going to be there to protect Paddy but if he could just instil in him enough confidence to stand up for himself, then at least he'd have achieved something.

Small and fit, Paddy gradually emerged from his melancholy reverie with Mervyn's help and began to assert himself, albeit in a subtle manner; he was still conscious of incurring the wrath of the Belfast boys.

He took on a job on the Lisburn Road near Finaghy, just ten minutes from the home, where he sewed sacks for potatoes. He was at last becoming more like the rest of the lads: he had a job and money to go out, and he was slowly building his independence. With the towering Mervyn by his side he enjoyed his new-found freedom.

'I went out into the city at night, drinking and socialising. There was no transport. We weren't really allowed to but we kept it under wraps from the Reverend Gilmore. That was the first time I had a drink. There was a quare difference from the other homes. It was more relaxed; it wasn't as strict as the other places.'

Mervyn, too, enjoyed the freedom the home provided. The prevailing ethos was that those in care were in need of support not punishment.

'We would have gone sometimes to see the Blues (Linfield soccer team) playing in Windsor Park. We could have come and gone as we pleased but we had to be in by 10pm. When we were in, we sat and watched TV, or when Reverend Thompson came, we could have sat and talked to him. He was good at handing cigarettes round for the boys to have a smoke.'

The real miracle and mercy for Paddy is that he did not become like the hardened boys who tormented him when he strayed across their path. Instead he found himself perpetually questioning why he had been thrown into a home with delinquents. Just as before in St Leonard's, he was confused; yet again he was perplexed at his misplacement.

'I never got into trouble then. That's why I always wondered why they put me in there. Had they nowhere else to put me? I was in there maybe a year. I got cheesed off with it.'

Mervyn left the home before Paddy's time there came to

an end. His mother had separated from her husband and Mervyn was able to return to Ballyclare in County Antrim, where he eventually settled down and started a family of his own. Of his large family of six sons and one daughter, Mervyn simply laughs and says, 'I was busy.'

Paddy and Mervyn were not to meet again for over thirty years when, by chance, Mervyn walked into a bar in Ballyclare where Paddy was treating the locals to a few tunes.

'I went into a pub one night and heard him singing. He had a lovely voice. He was a great chanter. We used to call him "P J Proby the Singer".'

Paddy was delighted with his new moniker. P J Proby from Houston, Texas, had started off singing with Baptist Gospel singers. He rose to fame in the early 1960s as a session singer for BB King, Johnny Cash, Little Richard and Elvis Presley and had a big hit with 'Try to Forget Her'. Paddy earned his nickname because he had the initials P J himself, but also because of a comical mishap the real P J Proby became renowned for on stage. In January 1965, while performing at Fairfield Hall in Croydon, London, Proby burst out of his skin tight velvet bellbottoms, much to the shock of the excited audience. He put the mishap down to poor material but when the same thing happened two days later and the audience went wild, a dim view was taken by the cardinals of British entertainment and Proby was swiftly banned from theatres across Britain. Paddy took great delight in being named after the mischievous songster and, indeed, it did his confidence no disservice to carry the provocative entertainer's title.

Paddy's last days in the Boys' Residential Home played out without incident. Although his guardian Mervyn was gone, Paddy was learning to fend for himself. He was also earning a living, and drinking and larking about with his friends. All the while he was absorbing the message that he was on his own and responsible for himself. He gradually let go of the thoughts that there was an incomplete family out there with a space just for him and that, one day, they might come looking for him. When somebody did come to see him shortly after the stabbing in the canteen, an unnerved Paddy told the Reverend Gilmore to send them away. As the years rolled by, the visitor he never met was forgotten.

5

ROCK 'N' ROLL swaggered into Belfast in the early sixties and by 1963 bars and cabaret clubs across the city were swinging to the sounds of Elvis Presley, Tom Jones and the Beatles. Short skirts, beehive hairdos and wild colours flooded the streets, paraded on the bodies of confident young women who had it and were not afraid to flaunt it — at least out of sight of their mothers. Men greased their hair back and practiced moves and lines to woo women on the dance floors of social clubs and bars. A cover version of Elvis's 'Kiss Me Quick' by the Royal Showband topped the charts. The showband era was going strong and groups were shaking, rattling and rolling dance halls up and down the country, determined to give people a good time.

Things were shaking up for Paddy too. He had moved out of the Boys' Residential Home on Blacks Road and in with the Rankin family on Henderson Avenue, in the shadow of the Cave Hill, in the north of the city. Harold Rankin, the Honorary Secretary of the Polio Fellowship, was a heavy smoker and a burly, good-natured man with short, wavy, fair hair. He had known Paddy for more than four years, since his time in Stewart Memorial. He had taken a shine to him and wanted to make Paddy's transition into adult life as smooth as possible. There was little support from social services when Paddy's time in care drew to a close and, afraid and alone, he was unsure as to what to do. The other lads in the home were self-assured and had long been planning the escape to their own digs but Paddy was filled with trepidation. So he was only too grateful when Harold offered a helping hand. When he joined Harold, his wife Margaret and their two young daughters, Joyce and Adrianne, in their home, he felt for the first time in his life that he was a part of what he had spent years longing for — a family. He knew it was only a temporary arrangement but to have a secure place to live in meant an awful lot to the teenager. Harold had Paddy's best interests at heart and, what's more, Paddy trusted him implicitly. He gave Paddy the freedom to live as he wanted and only asked him to respect his home and family, which Paddy did unquestioningly. The security that family life gave him was a foundation from which he could start building his future.

'I never called Harold Rankin by his first name in my life; it was always Mr Rankin,' Paddy says. 'Even his wife was "Mrs Rankin" when I lived with them. She was a lovely wee woman. She used to stand with her fag hanging out of her mouth in the kitchen while she cooked the steaks. Harold was a big, fat man. He had two sticks. It always used to amaze me how the man could walk. When he came down the stairs in the morning he came down on his backside. He would stand and put one of the sticks at his backside and lean on it while he was talking to you.'

With Harold as his guardian and a loving place to call home, Paddy did not have to always watch his back or be secretive with his possessions as he did when he was in care. He was happier and less hesitant about venturing out on his own. One thing that could be said of Paddy, though, was that he was a constant source of entertainment, whether intentionally or not.

During these carefree days of making friends and heading out on the town, Paddy commenced singing again. The last time he had sung in public was at the Gospel meetings at the Pickie Pool in Bangor when he was a child. But he loosened up his vocal chords once again for the customers and staff at the Bar 40, a long, narrow public house on the corner of Mountpottinger Road and the Albertbridge Road in east Belfast.

'When I was in my teens I was very, very shy. It wasn't until I started singing in the Bar 40 with the band, and meeting Eddie (McCrory), that I started coming out of myself. When I worked in the factories I didn't really bother with anybody. It wasn't until I got out into society that I really started to take up singing again. Paddy Hunt owned the Bar 40. There was a main bar downstairs but we were always upstairs. People from the Short Strand and the Cregagh area frequented it — Catholics and Protestants. There was no trouble in those days.'

Eddie's mother, Alice, worked there as a barmaid and, while she was popular with the customers, she would not tolerate untoward behaviour. Paddy recalls that he was in the pub enjoying a drink one night, when, as was the custom, after the group performed for a while, they invited patrons to sing. The group were impressed with Paddy's strong voice and invited him up to sing with them.

'They called me up for a song and that's when it started. The band that was playing — the Dollars, they came from Ligoniel in north Belfast — they were the resident band in the Bar 40 every Wednesday night but they were also residents on Monday nights in a bar in Victoria Square in the city centre. Later on we used to play Saturday nights up the Castlereagh Road at the social club of the toy factory.'

Paddy found a new lease of life and renewed confidence when he was singing. He had once used singing as a release to escape from his troubles at Stewart Memorial but now he was taking to the stage in bars where people came to hear him and he loved nothing better than to please them. Things were turning around: he had found a niche and was finally fitting in. His time in care had drawn to a close and he was his own man with no one to stand in his way or tell him what to do. He had his life laid out in front of him and he was finally finding some direction and enjoying it.

Despite his newfound confidence while performing, once off stage Paddy felt unsteady and nervous when it came to mixing with his peers. Sheepishly inching his way into adulthood, he lacked the sure-footedness other teens around him seemed to carry off with ease. But beneath all his insecurities Paddy possessed a fighting spirit and dogged determination which propelled him on to take risks where previously he'd cowered in fear of embarrassment. A little bit of gusto would rear its head every now and then, surprising Paddy himself, but giving him that extra push to take baby steps forward in building up his self-confidence. When it came to girls Paddy had little experience of talking to them, let alone propositioning them. So, one day, when a girl agreed to a date, Paddy took it for granted, as most hot-blooded males would, that she was genuinely interested in him.

'I was always very shy about asking girls out,' he says. 'I remember my first date was with one of the girls who worked behind the counter in the Wimpey Bar in Wellington Place. I used to go in there every day. She had a nice pleasant face and long, black hair. When I went in, she was in her uniform, a kind of striped outfit. I used to get milkshakes — that was the strongest they were allowed to serve you.'

Paddy and the girl seemed to hit it off, so they arranged to see each other at the Robinson and Cleaver store, a city centre landmark and popular meeting place. In eager anticipation, a spruced-up Paddy turned up as arranged outside the building on the corner of Donegall Place and Donegall Square North, opposite Belfast City Hall. From his vantage point on the corner he had a clear view straight down Donegall Place and on to Royal Avenue as it curved towards the north of the city. With his back to the building he gazed expectantly up Wellington Place, where the statue of Presbyterian firebrand preacher Henry Cooke stood at the far end looking back at him. Straggling shoppers and homeward-bound workers merged into one heaving mass. One group exhausted by the fight to get through the day, the other by the battle to claim their booty; both anxious to get back to their loved ones and share their tales and spoils. All oblivious to Paddy. He stepped backwards into the street and craned his neck up towards the clock atop the Robinson and Cleaver building. It was 6pm. He was on time. He returned to his waiting post and shuffled uneasily from foot to foot. His stomach growled a long, exaggerated rumble like a tiger cub's yawn. He was ravenous; he hadn't been able to eat before he left the house, and his nerves were getting the better of him. He straightened his tie, smoothed down his jacket and waited.

'Well, like an eejit, I stood there for about two hours. I only realised she had stood me up when Mickey Campbell (a friend) came along and said to me, "You fecking eejit, you only stand for ten minutes and then you leave." I never saw her again. I was always too scared to go back into the Wimpey. So that was my experience. I never had many girlfriends. That put me off. I used to go to the Plaza Ballroom with Mickey. I enjoyed it. I was able to dance and jive in those days. The swinging sixties were good. Plenty of drinking and you couldn't see yourself for smoke in the bars.'

Paddy's luck with women took a turn for the better with his friend Eddie McCrory's sister, Teresa, whom Paddy knew always had a soft spot for him, although this is something he conveniently forgets until Eddie jolts his memory.

'You asked her for a date and she met you on the Albertbridge Road at Jimmy Feely's shop. Teresa told me she thinks it was a Polio Fellowship dance you went to,' Eddie helpfully reminds him. 'Sure the last time she saw you she didn't know you because she remembered you as being skinny. She went over to William and she said, "I didn't recognise you, Paddy", and he said, "That's because I'm not. That's Paddy over there."'

The memory has the pair howling with laughter. Teresa did recall that she and Paddy had a brief romance when they were young and innocent.

'We met at the Polio Fellowship but I didn't know him awful well. We went out once or twice. We were very young at the time. I think I was about sixteen or seventeen.'

Teresa confesses that she was drawn in by Paddy's good looks and his 'lovely hair'. She said he was quite shy but that didn't discourage her.

'He was very good looking. He was very, very thin. I think there was a bit of a natural kink in his hair if I remember rightly. He was a bit shy, but likeable as well. It wasn't anything extraordinary but we had a nice time.'

Paddy's difficulty with walking did not register with Teresa, something she puts down to being so used to her brother's own disabilities.

'It never struck me. I think we actually danced a jive at one of the Fellowship dances,' she says.

Although their romance was fleeting, Teresa says she always thought of Paddy fondly.

'It was short; short but sweet,' she says. 'But I always remembered Paddy.'

Being best friends with Eddie, Paddy was never far from Teresa's door, even after their relationship ended.

'My family has been intertwined with Paddy for years,' Eddie says.

Being so near to a family, yet not being a part of it, was something Paddy felt keenly. Relationships were never easy for him and while being welcomed into Eddie's family was, on the one hand a wonderful experience, on the other it reminded Paddy just how alone in the world he was.

'Whatever Stewart Memorial did for me, and I think William's the same, we didn't bother with anybody,' he claims. 'No guidance, no mates to show you the respectable way to go about dating women. That's absolutely true. No big brothers and sisters. That's what I missed terribly. Eddie had all his family. I think that's why I'm like this today. It's just mind-boggling.'

Paddy was settling nicely into his new home with the Rankins, so Harold set about finding a steady job for him. He was friendly with the managing director of Camco Ltd, which manufactured equipment for the oil and gas industry at Whitehouse in Newtownabbey. Harold had no problem assuring him that Paddy would be an exemplary employee. He started on general labouring jobs and went on to spend the next twenty years with the company. House and job sorted, Paddy could get on with the business of enjoying life. But, just as everything seemed to be going swimmingly, Paddy's feet began causing him problems. Increasing pain in his toes was hampering his ability to walk. In mid-November 1963, he was taken into Musgrave Park Hospital to have further corrective surgery to try to resolve the problem. Paddy's marker for his stay in hospital was the assassination of President John F Kennedy on 22 November. The murder in broad daylight in Dallas, Texas, rocked the world and particularly Ireland, where the president had been a visitor just five months previously. Because of his Irish ancestry, Ireland looked fondly on President Kennedy and felt the loss keenly.

'I remember lying in hospital when he was assassinated. I was watching television in the ward when the news came on. It didn't really mean much to me but there was shock in the ward.'

When Paddy left hospital in early 1964, Harold suggested that it would help his mobility and independence if he had his own car. Invalid cars were readily available to people with disabilities and the three-wheeler was a life-saver for Paddy.

'I couldn't wait to get my car. Harold kept telling me to be patient. I did my driving test on a route in Duncairn Gardens in north Belfast. The examiner told me to carry out an emergency stop. He said he would hit the dashboard with his hand and I had to stop quickly. I nearly put him through the window. It was the old two-stroke engine and it was a dark blue colour. They were called invalid tricycles, but the first ones were the two-stroke. They were a godsend. They had three wheels. Very noisy, with sliding doors; the way the doors worked, you pushed them out first and then you slid them back. Sometimes if you pushed them too far they fell off.'

Paddy and Eddie revert to teenagers, competing with each other to prove who had the best vehicle.

'Did yours have the roof that came down?' Eddie inquires, pretending innocence.

'Solid roof,' Paddy returns.

'Mine had the roof that came down — a convertible,' Eddie says, erupting into laughter.

'Nothing but the best for McCrory,' Paddy retorts with a chuckle.

'Before Harold ever got the polio van, he drove a wee two-stroke himself. It was a two-tone colour and it was as noisy as hell. When I lived with him he used to park the polio van outside the house.'

It was in that van that Paddy had his first legitimate cigarette, bestowed on him by Harold Rankin.

"It was my twenty-first birthday. We were down in Bangor doing a collection for the Polio Fellowship and he said there's a packet of cigarettes for you. I'll always remember that they were Gallaher's Blues, untipped. I had been smoking lightly before that but I was always afraid of him seeing me.'

Harold had been a good friend and guardian to Paddy, steering him on the right road, the only father figure he had ever had. But by 1965 it was time for the twenty-one-year-old to fly the Rankins' nest and stand on his own two feet.

'He and the wife and the two daughters were very

supportive to me. Only for Harold I would have been a delinquent or put in jail or done something stupid. He kept me out of trouble and kept me sane. Everything I learned, I learned from him. Harold was an authoritative figure to everybody. You did what he told you. I'm very grateful to the Northern Ireland Polio Fellowship.'

With Harold's help Paddy found digs with a lady called Charlotte Barber at Palestine Street, in the Holylands area of south Belfast.

Charrlotte, or 'Shaddy' to all who knew her, was a polio survivor herself and a member of the Polio Fellowship. She lived with her husband, Sam, who was a gardener by trade, although his own front garden measured less than two feet wide and three in length and his back 'garden' was an encased, paved-over yard.

'Shaddy was a case,' Eddie recalls. 'She used to frighten the life out of you. She would say, "Come on in here 'til I kiss you; oh, I could kiss you lovely." I was only eleven or twelve and I was like, "What's going to happen to me?"'

Paddy moved into the two-up, two-down, brown-bricked terrace which was packed neatly in a row of identical tidy, little houses. The poky and dark terrace in the inner city and predominantly working class area of the Ormeau Road was a striking change from the suburbs of north Belfast and Harold's roomy home. It was, however, a change that Paddy relished. Queen's University was only a five-minute walk around the corner and the area was teeming with students who mingled freely with families in the area. Stepping out his front door Paddy was immediately immersed in the hustle and bustle of city life with neighbours shouting greetings to each other across the street.

'Good morning, Mrs Barber.'

'Mornin', Mrs Martin. Shocking weather we're having.'

The very life-blood of the city, the River Lagan, flowed unhindered through the arches under the Ormeau Bridge, just yards from Paddy's house, flirting with the heart of the city, abruptly swerving in the direction of the docks and spilling out into Belfast Lough. Paddy was enjoying his new-found freedom and, with his trusty three-wheeler revved up, there was no stopping him. He could go wherever he wanted, when he wanted, provided of course that he could afford to put fuel in the tank. His singing career was taking off too. He had become a regular drinker and performer in the Bar 40 and was a well-known character and songster in bars across the city. This independence was a breath of fresh air which filled Paddy with vitality and a self-belief he had never experienced before.

'Singing was an outlet. I met a lot of people, very interesting people,' he says.

Among those he met in the unassuming Bar 40 were regulars Dickie and Ann Best from the Cregagh estate in east Belfast and, occasionally, their teenage son, George.

Nineteen-year-old George Best was an established footballer in 1965 when he and Paddy first met. Having been snapped up by a scout for the Old Trafford Club in 1961 at the age of fifteen, George, or 'Geordie', as Paddy knew him, was the hottest football talent the soccer world had seen in years. He left his parent's mid-terrace house in Burren Way to join one of England's top soccer clubs, Manchester United. It was in September 1963, at the age of seventeen, that George made his first division debut against West Bromwich Albion. By the time he and Paddy crossed paths this footballing genius was already taking the soccer world by storm.

Paddy was also making a name for himself as a singer, albeit on a far smaller scale. In addition to his regular stints in the Bar 40, he had picked up bookings for the Shorts Social Club on Sunday nights — another favourite with the Bests.

'I frequented the bar well before Geordie started coming in. But his mother and father were regulars and I got to know them first. Then, when Geordie came over, I caught up with him. Geordie's mother and father went to the Shorts Club on a Sunday night. If Geordie was back in the city, he would have come as well.'

With only two years separating them, Paddy and George were two young men with similar personalities and not altogether used to the adulation celebrity brought with it.

'I was like George, shy and all that. He was a very quiet fellow. We got on all right. We mostly talked about football. But I didn't see him as a famous person and I think that's what he appreciated. The Bar 40 was the sort of bar he could come into where he wasn't hassled; everybody knew him and his parents. He signed autographs, but even in the Shorts Social Club he didn't have any bother. I went to his house in Burren Way and I got on well with his sisters. Dickie used to invite me up for a cup of tea.'

Paddy got on so well with the Best family that on several occasions Dickie took him over to visit George in his digs in Manchester.

'He was quite famous at the time. I remember I went to his lodgings with Dickie a few times. We went to matches and had a meal with George afterwards. George took us to meet Patricia Phoenix and Bill Roache from *Coronation Street* in a bar in Manchester. I was star-struck in those days, meeting all these people. We had a few drinks of course.

Geordie didn't drink too much in those days. He was a very easy-going chap. I got on splendidly with him, with me not treating him as a star. He couldn't drink much because he had to be in bed by a certain time with the football and so on. I don't remember him drinking until later on.

'He drove the white Jaguar at the time. Quite distinctive. It was great. I was delighted to have a run in it.'

On the same visit to Manchester, Paddy met another Manchester United star, and friend of George's — David Sadler. This was a dream come true for Paddy. While he had long ago put fantasies of being a footballer behind him, here he was in the presence of two of the game's greatest players. He couldn't have been happier.

'Sadler was the centre-half of Man United then. He was a great friend of Geordie's. Geordie took us out to dinner with him. It was great craic. I thought I was one of the boys.'

Returning to Belfast and his own career, Paddy was very grateful for the encouraging words George's parents gave to him in pursuing his singing.

'Dickie and Ann used to say to me, "Wee man, you should go further. You're a great wee singer." It was they who introduced me to the Shorts Club.'

In the course of the six or seven years that Paddy and George shared an acquaintance, George's career went from strength to strength. His art of weaving in and out through players on the pitch left the defence dizzy and confused, his majestic presence sometimes enough in itself to leave the opposition floundering. His prominence in Manchester United helped to bring the team success in 1965 and 1967 with league titles. In 1968 George scored in an historic match which made his team the first English side to achieve European Cup glory. That same year saw him collect the

European Footballer of the Year trophy. These two Belfast men set out with dazzling futures but both their careers would be cut short by an overdependence on alcohol.

Paddy's first significant success on the music circuit was winning a talent competition in the Orpheus Ballroom at York Street, near Belfast city centre.

'The competition was held away up the stairs. They had a lift — it was one of those old-time lifts and the man in it only had one arm and always sat on a stool. The talent competition went on for about five or six weeks and there were heats. It was a knock-out and we took part each week. Jimmy Johnston was the compere.'

It was in the Orpheus that Paddy first met Gloria Hunniford, a talented young singer who was to go on to become a prominent television personality. Although Gloria at the time was considered to be a very good singer with excellent prospects, she did not win that particular competition.

'I remember sitting on the stool singing Dickie Rock's "Every Step of the Way" and Englebert Humperdink's "Please Release Me". A fellow called Noel Thompson, from the Shankill Road, and myself tied for first place in the competition. We had to share it because they couldn't decide on a winner. The prize was £1,000, which was a fair bit of money. The entertainment journalist, Eddie McIlwaine, wrote an article in the *Belfast Telegraph* about it, saying, "This man could go on if he concentrates on it."'

For the next few years Paddy did the rounds in Belfast and shared the stage with many up-and-coming stars. These included Roy Walker, who was to become a popular comedian and, later, presenter of the television game-show *Catchphrase*.

'Roy was the compere in the Talk of the Town. He sang a bit as well,' Paddy recalls.

Paddy is not very forthcoming about his time on stage, too modest to reveal that he regularly featured well up the billing. But Eddie has no hesitation in recalling his friend's promising career at the Talk of Town at Bridge End, close to where the M3 motorway link is now.

'To sing in the Talk of the Town was big. It was the main place for attracting the big English stars. You had made it if you were invited to sing at Bridge End,' Eddie says.

Paddy adds, 'That's where I met Carl Denver, an American country and western singer. He was over for a week doing a show in the Talk of the Town. I went to those places intending to learn the trade, but my problem was that I was very nervous when I got on stage. I had to have four or five vodkas inside me. I had a bit of banter between songs but it was more nerve-wracking than the singing.'

In 1966 Paddy moved ten doors down from Shaddy Barber's house to 33 Palestine Street to live with Mrs Herron and her husband, Victor. Mrs Herron's son, Victor junior, had polio and Paddy had stayed with the family on several occasions during his time in Stewart Memorial. It was many years since the wild days when Paddy ran away from Stewart Memorial to Mrs Herron's door for refuge and refused to leave. Mrs Herron saw that Paddy had matured into a 'lovely young man' and she was delighted to put him up for a while. Her husband, on the other hand, was a different matter. Paddy's stay with the Herrons was cut short because he and Mr Herron couldn't see eye to eye.

'I didn't get on with her husband. When I was in Palestine Street with Mrs Herron I used to go to the wee pubs with her. The Errigle Inn — that was a lovely pub. We used to go in there and I sometimes sang there with groups like the Dollars.'

The worsening relationship between Paddy and Mr Herron made it impossible for Paddy to continue living with the family and, in 1967, Paddy was on the move again, this time to the opposite side of the city and the Shankill Road. North, south, east and now west of the city, Paddy's personal compass led him from area to area oblivious to the tensions bubbling below the surface. By 1967 these tensions were coming to the fore with unionists and loyalists fighting among themselves, and nationalists making strides in asserting their civil rights. But Paddy was a stranger among the men who were looking to settle old grievances. He had no interest in politics and had learned during his time in care to keep his head down and keep out of trouble. While young men of Paddy's age met in pubs along the Shankill Road to lay plans to take on the IRA, he moved into the area to escape previous unhappy dwellings and wanted no part in their plans. His new landlady, Aggie McMurray, was an elderly soul who made the tea at the Polio Fellowship meetings in Polio House on the Antrim Road. She lived on Matchett Street, just off the Shankill Road, and was only too happy to get Paddy out of a jam.

'When I was stuck she put me up for a while. I wasn't there very long. It was a wee parlour house. There was a curtain at the bottom of the stairs. There was no banister and I had to crawl up the stairs, but I was young and fit then. Just next door was Tommy McFall's pub and she always sent me in there for her cigarettes.'

Aggie doted on Paddy, and the two often sat beside the coal fire in her parlour having a yarn and a smoke and whiling the hours away.

'It was an old coal fire she had in those days and we sat round it, smoking and talking. She had no stockings on and she sat that close to the fire that her legs regularly got burned or measled as we called it. That cough of hers was terrible. It was a wonder I took smoking up. She was an oul gurn but she was very, very good. I got on great with her.'

Paddy left his job in Camco after five years to move to Everton Engineering, which was also on Church Road in Newtownabbey.

'I worked at Everton for about a year. They made big tanks. I was a buffer and used a big brush to clean all the scales off the metal. They made hospital trolleys too.'

The work was labour intensive and very tiring and it wasn't long before Paddy fell ill with dermatitis. He took a few months off sick and, when he recovered, he returned to Camco. By 1968 he had also returned to his old hunting ground in the south of the city. The house, number 185A, fronted on to the Ormeau Road. It had six steps leading up to its front door but had a hand-rail on one side which enabled Paddy to clamber up. He had rented one of the flats in the boarding house from Mrs Elliott. Her husband, George Billy, worked for the council as a meter reader, while she took care of the lodgers and lodgings. Living just around the corner, in Agincourt Avenue, was Elizabeth Wright, another member of the Polio Fellowship. Paddy became friendly with Miss Wright, a spinster in her sixties, through the meetings in Polio House. But it was her brother's fame that has kept her to the fore of Paddy's memory.

'She was Jackie Wright's sister. Jackie was the wee baldy man on the Benny Hill shows on television and Benny always used to smack his head. I watched him all the time on the show.'

Paddy, meanwhile, was plugging away at his singing career, trying to achieve some fame for himself. He was working in Camco during the day and doing the rounds of the bars at night. Supported by the in-house band, he played to packed cabaret clubs. The reaction from the crowds was great. They loved his voice and he would have them on their feet dancing in no time with little bother and a bit of banter to boot.

'I worked in the Ulster Waltz Club. That's where I met Frank Carson. And there was a wee jazz place, I can't remember the name of, but I never liked it much. I also sang at a couple of Camco dinners.'

Praise and drinks were flowing in Paddy's direction and his friends urged him to try to make it to the big time. He had a booming, deep voice that stopped punters mid-sip and sent shivers up their spines as he covered the chart-topping hits by the big singers of the day.

'"Son, you're a great wee singer." That's what they told me,' he recalls.

In the spring of 1970 one of Paddy's friends heard about an audition for the Thames Television talent show *Opportunity Knocks* and coaxed Paddy into going along. After much persuasion, a bashful Paddy gave in and crossed the Irish Sea to Stranraer to audition for the show.

'A mate from the Shore Road came over with me, a guy called Winky Cairns. Hughie Green was the host of the show.'

Paddy sang his heart out. It was all he had ever wanted to be, a professional singer like his idols. He returned home after his audition and waited for a reply. It was a long time coming and, when it did arrive in June, it wasn't good news.

'I got a letter not to actually go on the show but for the

heats. Len Marten was the executive producer who signed the letter and it basically said the same thing as Eddie McIlwaine's review, "Keep trying, polish up your act and you could come back to this with a real chance."'

It was a knock-back but the words of encouragement gave Paddy reason for some optimism. He loved singing and wanted nothing more than to make a go of it and become a star. He wasn't lacking in passion or talent but, to the aesthetically-obsessed television world, the visible evidence of polio was a glaring impediment to any future in entertainment.

'What held me back was my disability — that's why I didn't get on. I had a half and a full calliper and it would have been obvious from the way I walked. When you wear a full calliper you can't bend your leg at all, it's locked. The man told me in Stranraer anyone with a disability would be discriminated against. He said, "You don't get many disabled people at auditions."'

Paddy was devastated. The only thing he had ever been praised for and respected for in his own right was his voice and now his disability was standing between him and the future he wanted.

'I took that to heart and never concentrated enough on the singing. I think if I had got a good agent and really worked... In England there were a lot of agents but we didn't really have that in Northern Ireland. I never bought a record in my life. I heard the songs on the radio and then went to these shows and listened to people singing them and I picked them up that way, mostly ballads by all the famous singers of the day.'

It was his first major setback on the road to a rock 'n' roll lifestyle but, unfortunately, Paddy wasn't feeling ready to bounce back and give it a second go. If it was his disability that was holding him back, then there was nothing he could about it, so why bother?

He would just put his head down and keep playing to the audiences who appreciated his voice regardless of his disability and that would have to be enough. It was just another blow to his confidence and Paddy was getting used to those by now.

6

FAME MAY NOT have been exactly beckoning but Paddy soon found an up side to being a big fish in a little pond — women. He was getting plenty of female attention, something he wasn't used to, but something he was quite prepared to take advantage of. As most ladies will admit, there is something very alluring about a man who can sing. Add to that a sense of humour and you're on to a winner. Paddy had both on stage and before long he had the ladies throwing themselves at his feet. He was no Mick Jagger but there was an ample supply of young women only too eager to share a drink and a flirt, and the hope of something more, with the twenty-six-year-old Paddy when he had finished his set.

'I got a lot of female interest when I was singing but I was more interested in the music. Half the time I was blocked anyway,' he admits. 'All I ever drank was vodka and lemonade. I never took to Guinness or beer. I had gin once but it sent me crazy, I thought I was Elvis or something.'

And did he take up any of the ladies' offers? Paddy grins and says, 'No comment.'

'One had an enjoyable time,' he adds mischievously. 'It was good old craic. I was shy and I was half-blocked. When I was half-blocked I thought I was a better singer.'

Whether he was a better singer or not is something that is open to debate. There is no doubt he enjoyed his time in the spotlight, and there was the added bonus of meeting women whom he was generally too shy to approach if on a night out. He was self-conscious about his disability but also quite reserved, so singing, and drinking, energised him enough to give him the confidence to pursue the ladies.

'I met them in different clubs. There were plenty of one-night stands. When I was up singing, they were coming in saying, "There is my heart-throb tonight again." They weren't knocking you down or anything, but you felt great, you felt as if you were important. They said, "You're a great oul singer", and I used to be very shy and nervous and generally said, "Catch yourselves on."'

Shy or not Paddy had plenty of success with his admiring female fans and took to 'kerfuffling' with little hesitation. 'That's what we called it in those days, "kerfuffling" — courting,' he laughs.

However, Paddy's reputation as a crooner had cause to land him in trouble. One night when he was out singing at a function for some friends he found himself on the receiving end of a smack in the face.

'I was singing in a bar on Clifton Street on Christmas Eve. A young girl I knew from the Polio Fellowship, her parents were celebrating their twenty-fifth wedding anniversary. She was only fourteen, so she wasn't there. I went over to say hello to the family and congratulate her sister who had just got engaged but her boyfriend was very jealous and punched me. I went straight down. The family were very embarrassed and invited me back to their house for a drink. So it didn't turn out to be a bad night after all.'

Courting was one thing, but love was a different matter altogether. Paddy is very reticent about revealing anything about his relationships. He is adamant that he was never in love.

'No. That was the whole problem, I never could be. The homes and the lifestyle made a nervous wreck out of me. I went out with about four or five women but I could never get attached to anybody. That was my whole problem throughout my life. All my relationships were short-term. Most of them wouldn't have lasted longer than a year.'

While he has no hesitation in revealing that he soon tired of the 'one-night stands', Paddy recoils when it comes to discussing his relationships in any depth.

'All my mates went out with different women and had a good time but I was always shy with women. They treated women like dirt, but I didn't. I treated women like ladies and my friends couldn't understand this. They said that's where I went wrong and all that sort of crap.

'I remember two or three girlfriends asking me, "Do you not love me?" I said, "No", and I explained to them about the homes in Bangor and they understood. When I had a girlfriend I didn't see it going very far.

'The homes in Bangor totally destroyed me in that respect. It's the way it panned out,' he says with the air of a man reconciled to bachelorhood. 'I think it would still happen to this day. For a lot of disabled people like me, when you're out and you're chatting up women, they don't seem to want to know, unless you meet the right women.'

Where the 'right women' may be found, Paddy is unsure, and he has no expectations of finding one at this stage in his life. His disability, if not immediately obvious while on stage, soon became apparent when he was on the singing circuit. But it was his emotional and not physical handicap that held him back from a meaningful relationship with a woman. This is another thing his upbringing in care robbed him of. He was never in one place long enough to maintain a friendship for a lengthy period of time and never had a sustained relationship with a maternal figure as a guide on how to nurture an emotional attachment to a woman.

The impermanence of most of his relationships, and the lack of a firm foundation of appropriate behaviour, saw him reaching a certain point in relationships and then withdrawing. He was constantly looking over his shoulder to his childhood and what he had missed out on. This preoccupation with the unresolved issues of his past blocked any paths to his future.

'I am more open now,' he says. 'In those days I was more interested in my childhood — I've been in transitional periods ever since. I'm convinced, at sixty-two, I am hitting my peak but I have no intention of getting into a relationship, I'm too settled in my ways. It sounds awfully selfish but I am. I can't see me going out with a woman and moving into another place.'

Moving is a thorny issue for Paddy as he has spent most of his life moving unwillingly from pillar to post. The thought of being uprooted again for whatever reason is a cause of great anxiety to him.

His mother's desertion has had a profound effect on his relationships. Her disappearance, coupled with his disability, left him feeling that he had started out in life as a lesser person, with ground to make up. He didn't have the benefit of loving parents to show him that he was perfect to them no matter how 'imperfect' he felt himself.

Paddy adapted to his circumstances by shielding himself from potential harm and he confesses that he always felt more at ease when he was alone. Not having a long-term girlfriend was not something he really spent time brooding over. He was too busy putting his own life together to worry about whether or not he had a woman by his side.

Paddy learned to live his life in this guarded manner but his defensiveness is understandable for a man who, from childhood, matured into adulthood with nobody to call family and no place to call home. He had nobody to rely on but himself and had to create his own home, but the more he fought to survive the more he alienated himself from those who were willing to share his life. He wouldn't allow anything into his life that could penetrate his armour: when a relationship started getting serious he jumped ship. Paddy finds it difficult to put into words why he never pursued a romance and is visibly uncomfortable at any probing into this area of his life. He simply says that his mother's desertion had a big part to play in how he felt towards women.

'It felt alright to have a girlfriend but I still had no confidence in myself. It didn't really annoy me if I didn't have a girlfriend. I had my own life to put together. I had to find all my jobs; I didn't need anybody to hold my shoulder up. It didn't annoy me. I was a loner. I'm still a loner to this day. I enjoy people's company but I can't have anybody talking nonsense to me. I suppose most people can't. I don't know how to put it. It was very much to do with my mum, very much so. I suppose I just didn't trust women.'

There was very little warning for Paddy's girlfriends

when he felt the liaison had run its course. They were lucky to get a brief explanation and a 'see you around'.

'I wasn't rude or anything. I just said, "No it's not working out. Bye, see you again."'

The heady mix of booze and women Paddy became used to at twenty-six lured him into a hectic lifestyle of nocturnal living, heading out after work to bars and partying into the wee small hours. He started relying on alcohol to buoy him up and iron out his nerves before he went on stage.

'I had to have a drink in me before I went up — my nerves were wrecked. Sometimes I was physically sick. I found it was a ruthless game, entertaining; you were on your own, you had to fight your way, every man for himself. At times, it did and again it didn't feel great to be on stage. When it was bad, I thought, "They're not listening to me sing, they're just looking at me and my disability." If the perks had been better I would have been flying but my disability definitely held me back.'

The drink and the women were certainly perks but not enough to make it worthwhile. The money barely covered the cost of Paddy's reliance on countless vodkas and lemonade. It was time to take the plunge and try his hand at the music scene in England.

In the summer of 1971, Paddy set off for the place in England he was most familiar with: Manchester. It had been over five years since he had last set foot in the city; then it had been to visit George Best but this time he was alone. George was a big star on the football field and had been making a name for himself off the field too, being quite the ladies' man.

Impressed by George's success, Paddy was savouring his own taste of glory. At twenty-six, for the first time in his life, he was striking out on his own with only the cash he had in his pocket and a vague plan to try to make it on the Manchester music scene. When he landed in the city he set about looking for labouring shifts to tide him over until he landed his first gig. However, work was thin on the ground, particularly for a disabled, Northern Irish 'blow-in'.

Doing the rounds of factories looking for employment he heard about some gigs in working men's clubs and decided to give them a shot. These were rough-and-ready places where Mancunian workers unwound with a few drinks after a long day of heavy labour.

As Paddy entered one club the scent of stale smoke and drink hung in the air. A fraternity of chain-smoking workmates had gathered around tables with overflowing ashtrays and greetings were shouted to fellow workers as they came through the door, gasping for pints of beer chased by shots of whiskey.

Eyes followed Paddy as he walked up to the bar to tell the barman he was booked to sing that evening.

'Take a seat there, lad. You'll be needing a drink,' the barman instructed him.

Paddy nodded. 'Vodka and lemonade.'

'All right there, son? Where you from then?' a small, sixty-something man with a Donegal accent asked Paddy as he took a long draw on a cigarette.

'Belfast,' Paddy replied, his nerves settling a little.

Having put in his training in the clubs of inner city Belfast, Paddy wasn't overly perturbed at having to impress this class of clientele. He had performed to his fair share of fickle audiences and was used to satisfying the tastes of hardened factory workers who demanded immediate gratification. So he was unfazed by the mean faces of the working-class Manchester men. These men had little tolerance for time-wasters. They were spending their hard-earned cash on as many drinks as they could before heading home for dinner to wives and screaming kids. Lesser men than Paddy had been given short shrift by this crowd of substantial hecklers, mouths loaded and ready to fire vitriolic words at half-assed performers.

As he took to the stage the men eyed him up suspiciously through the dense smoke-filled room, just waiting for him to slip up, waiting for the opportunity to boo him off.

A barman stood, hand poised on the knotted rope attached to the bell, waiting for the first signs of restlessness from the crowd. By ringing the bell he would be calling time on Paddy's act, and turfing him off the stage. They were a tough audience but Paddy was confident that he could win them over. Nerves sedated by three or four vodkas, he took a deep breath and launched into his opening number.

Being booed off stage meant you didn't get paid and, as his stints on stage were his only source of income, apart from occasional labouring shifts, he made sure he always got paid. 'Singing in the clubs was my only job. It paid for my lodgings, my drink and my cigarettes. The clubs were huge. If they didn't like the act, they would ring the bell and shout, "Get off, you bugger you!" They wouldn't have paid you if they didn't like you. But I always got paid. I never had a bell rung on me. I never had that problem. The money wasn't bad. I got about £20 a night, good enough money. £100 a week was some money in those days. It was great craic. I learned the ins-and-outs of the game and had plenty of banter with the guys.'

He survived and, more than that, was a hit with the crowd: at the end of the day, they all wanted to have a good night and Paddy, fuelled with drink himself, was ready and willing to join in the fun. After a few months he grew tired of making a living on a song and a smile. A lot of the other entertainers he met had agents who were ruthless when it came to getting their clients slots in clubs. He found it increasingly difficult to book a gig without being pipped at the post by some wily agent, but he couldn't afford the prices they demanded for management and was gradually squeezed off the line-up and out of the scene.

'I had no more interest in it. There were a lot of thugs. You had to employ an agent and then, after he got his cut, the money wasn't great. I was there for two or three months. I got fed up with it in the end, so I came home.'

Paddy came back to Belfast in the autumn of 1971, initially with his tail between his legs. He was, however, able to return to his old job at Camco with little hassle. He moved in with Shaddy Barber in Palestine Street for a few months because the Elliotts, whom he had been living with on the Ormeau Road, were moving house. Slotting back into his old way of life with relative ease, he was soon back in the same bars singing to the same crowds. This was what he enjoyed, being asked to sing a few songs and getting a couple of drinks in return — no agents, no pressure. He would play anywhere as long as there were a few drinks and maybe a few pounds at the end of the night.

But Belfast was much changed from the city he had first set foot in as a sixteen-year-old.

Northern Ireland was going through painful growing pains, with life as many knew it being turned on its head. An air of caution and unease had descended and the streets were no longer as safe as they once were. Political turmoil was unfurling around Paddy and he couldn't ignore the violence erupting in Belfast and across the whole of Northern Ireland.

A few years earlier, in 1968, the Civil Rights movement had been formed. Catholics, resentful of long years of discrimination, began to take action and joined protest marches in their thousands. But civil rights were not easily won. The American civil rights leader Martin Luther King had been assassinated in April of that year. A civil rights march in Derry on 5 October 1968 saw Northern Ireland enter into a new era of Troubles when the RUC confronted marchers, bludgeoning them with batons, in front of television cameras which relayed the images to the rest of the world.

The Troubles had begun.

In August 1969 the police took to the streets of Derry with tear gas after eight hours of street clashes and baton charges following a march through the city by the Apprentice Boys, an exclusively Protestant organisation. It was one of the worst periods of disturbances since the Troubles began but worse was yet to come. In Belfast two days later, two men and a nine-year-old boy were shot dead in what the media called 'the worst streets flare-up since the 1921 Troubles'. Catholic families in west Belfast were driven from their homes by Protestant extremists in Cupar Street, between the Falls Road and the Shankill Road, and their houses set on fire. The following night the nationalist Bombay Street and surrounding streets came under heavy sniper fire from the direction of the Shankill Road. The Falls Road was a scene of devastation the next day as a procession of refugees from the area carried what few possessions they could muster and made their way to the safety of schools and parish halls after threats of more violence. The very fabric of Northern Irish society was rapidly coming undone at the seams, spilling the blood and woes of its people on to the streets. Normal life in working class areas all but disappeared. There were, however, some bars and clubs which attempted to provide entertainment for their customers. In the midst of this violence Paddy was still trying to plough his way to perform in venues across the city.

'I sang through the start of the Troubles. It made me cautious. I was singing in the Hatfield Bar on the Ormeau Road, a nationalist area, and in bars up the loyalist Shankill Road. I was taking a chance in those days and was always afraid of something happening. People stayed in their own communities at that time. They were too afraid to go out.'

1972 was one of the worst years of violence the people of Northern Ireland were to witness. On 30 January, thirteen men were shot dead in Derry when the Parachute Regiment opened fire on participants of an illegal civil rights march against internment. Thirteen others were wounded, one of whom later died. Bloody Sunday, as the massacre was to become known, sent shockwaves throughout the north and south of Ireland, the UK and the rest of the world.

Later that year, Paddy moved from Shaddy Barber's house to the Elliotts' new residence on the Ormeau Road. The three-storey house was one of seven towering together in a row between the bottom of University Avenue and Fitzroy Avenue. The houses faced the Hatfield Bar, on the corner of Hatfield Street, a popular drinking spot with the Elliotts' lodgers.

'There were about seven or eight lodgers. The Lower

Ormeau area was very mixed in religious terms in those days. There were a couple of school teachers from Fermanagh in the house who I used to play cards with.'

It was during this period with the Elliotts that Paddy agreed to a suggestion that he join the Orange Order. The exclusively Protestant organisation was viewed by many Catholics as a sectarian organisation but Protestants regarded it as a cultural institution which allowed them to celebrate their history.

Paddy's membership of the Order was a departure for him given that he had shown no previous interest in aligning himself with either culture. Paddy had been christened Patrick Joseph, a sure indication of a Catholic background. His very Catholic forenames, however, failed to ring alarm bells when his application was received by officials of his local Orange Lodge. The move caused much hilarity among Paddy's acquaintances many years later when it was discovered that a 'half-Catholic' not only became a member of the Orange Order but took part in the organisation's annual Twelfth of July marches.

'Mr Elliott was a member of Ballynafeigh Orange Order and I was game for anything in those days. I'd have joined anything to be quite honest with you. It was a macho kind of thing. I thought it was the cool thing to do. So I joined, but it wasn't for very long.'

Because of his disability Paddy couldn't walk far without great difficulty, so when it came to the marches he didn't actually walk, but travelled in a limousine with senior officials of the Order. These vehicles were given pride of place at the front of the parade.

He was still working in Camco and had an invalid car to ferry himself across the town to work. Camco had moved premises from Church Road to Cloughern Avenue off the Doagh Road in Newtownabbey.

'I used to travel up and down through the Markets, a nationalist area of Belfast, when I was on the nightshift during the Troubles, when the bullets were flying. At the time of the Workers' Strike I drank in the Trocadero bar in the area. There was never any bother. I kept myself to myself and never talked to anybody. I was only in for a couple of drinks and then out again.'

The Ulster Workers' Council (UWC) strike in May 1974 was sparked in reaction to the establishment of a power-sharing executive at Stormont under the Sunningdale Agreement, which called for unionists and nationalists to sit in government together. The UWC was comprised of trade unionists and workers in the predominantly Protestant industries of shipbuilding, engineering and power stations. Roadblocks were set up across the city and manned by masked men set on intimidating workers from going to work. Loyalist dominance in the power stations meant power cuts could swiftly sweep across the city, forcing workplaces to close. Belfast was being held to ransom by an army of loyalists united in their aim to shut down the assembly. The UWC further demonstrated their power by blocking access to petrol to all but 'essential users'. Paddy was fortunate enough to be one of these.

'I was in Camco during the strike. We were practically locked in the factory for a week. People couldn't get out, couldn't manoeuvre about the streets. I travelled about in the invalid car; invalid drivers were among the few to get petrol during the strike. But you had to get out to earn a living. I was always looking about me as soon as I left the house. But once I got through the city and out towards the factory, it was fine.'

Dark clouds had descended over the north and, days after the strike started, the clouds erupted with three massive explosions in Dublin and a fourth in Monaghan. The bombs killed thirty-three people and injured hundreds of others. Responsibility for the carnage was laid at the door of the Ulster Volunteer Force.

Belfast's streets were overrun by loyalists, stirring up intimidation and fear. After two weeks such was the disorder and chaos on the streets that Stormont Prime Minister Brian Faulkner, regarded as 'too soft on nationalism and republicanism', gave in to loyalist pressure and resigned. The executive was subsequently dissolved. The strikers had achieved their aim.

As the community stumbled back to some semblance of normality, Paddy was back on the road and back to his singing. People were afraid to venture too far from home so Paddy travelled to clubs in their areas. His travels up the Shankill Road over the course of the Troubles in the mid-seventies took him into loyalist drinking dens, which were illegal but popular haunts for people afraid to stray from their area for a drink and a dance. In an atmosphere where caution reigned, strangers were immediate cause for suspicion. He was taking risks venturing out from the Ormeau Road and across the city to sing for a few pounds of drinking money but he did so nonetheless.

'I ended up singing in loyalist clubs: wee huts — prefabs, not very big, sometimes made out of corrugated tin. They were actually shebeens. The Shankill area was full of them. I got a tenner a set. It was drinking money. I felt safe enough. I got invited because I knew guys through work who frequented these places. I sang and played cards but I mostly drank in them.'

The pressure eventually took its toll on Paddy. He had been born a Catholic but knew little about this and was brought up as a Presbyterian. He had long ago fallen away from his faith and did not consider himself a Protestant or want to take sides in this sectarian war. Allegiances to one religion or the other did not mean anything to him, despite his brief fling with the Orange Order. But he knew the lay of the land and the instability of relations between Catholics and Protestants in the north's fragile infrastructure where trouble could ignite at a moment's notice.

'If I had to do it all again I definitely wouldn't. That was the ruining of me, going to those clubs. I was always on edge, even though I was singing in them. I didn't stay until the end of the night. I always had somewhere else to go. I used to pop in and out. I would do a set in two or three clubs in the one night. I had a few drinks in each place, though. The police knew the shebeens were operating but they didn't do much about them. I never changed my name but I was known as Joe Grimshaw in Camco. No one ever queried me because everybody knew the workmates I was with. The boys would say, "He's alright." They were all blocked (drunk) anyway. But I'll tell you, it was a different world up there. The only time I ever saw anything untoward was on the Shankill when a guy with a mask came in. He wasn't near me, he was round the back and he only stayed a few minutes. I just kept on singing.'

Paddy was never questioned about his religion but he was aware that he was the product of a mixed relationship, and that was something he knew the wrong people could take issue with.

'It was always at the back of my mind. It made me nervous. But I think, because of my disability, it made me stand out; a lot of people knew me through the grapevine, so there was no problem.'

Religion occupied Paddy's mind on a personal level as well.

'It always tore me to pieces. I know I was brought up as a Protestant but it was always in the back of my mind that my parents were in a mixed marriage. All my life I was wondering whether my parents were this or that. I was in turmoil to find out where I came from, how I got here, how I got there.'

Paddy didn't have his birth certificate to quell his doubts and wasn't to see it until a number of years later, in 1982. It was probably just as well he didn't have access to it during the highly unstable and sensitive years of the Troubles, or he may have been reluctant to set foot in the loyalist areas where he was a regular. Indeed, had Paddy realised at the time that he was in fact the son of a Catholic woman from the nationalist Falls Road, he may also have thought twice about joining the Orange Order. As it was he was none the wiser and no worse off for his ignorance. His lifestyle of working during the day and then doing the rounds of the shebeens at night continued. Before long he got into a routine of moving from club to club and joining in with the heavy drinking that went with the turf.

'It was some craic in those days, we had some laughs. When I was playing in those clubs I would have a drink before the show, during and after. Once I hit the club that was it — I had the first drink and didn't stop until I left the club at one or half-past one in the morning. Sometimes I went back to one of the boys' houses for a bit of a party and didn't get to bed until three or four o'clock.'

One night, after a round with the heavyweight drinkers in the shebeens, Paddy climbed into his invalid car and made for home. He traversed the whole way across town without incident and was within one hundred yards of his house when a wary bunch of policemen spotted his trusty three-wheeler trundling unsteadily up the road.

The 'cripple cars' were notoriously unstable, even for a sober driver. With just three wheels, a sharp turn could cause the vehicle to keel over. Having a driver under the influence certainly didn't help. Paddy was 'three sheets to the wind' and in no fit state to be in a parked car, never mind pelting up the road in his two-stroke. Looking back, Paddy admits he was very foolish but said he soon sobered up when he was ordered out of his chariot by the unhappy police squad.

'The police arrested me there and threw me in the back of the wagon and took me down to Musgrave Police Station. I was brought before the law courts down there. The magistrate was wearing a Pioneer pin (a religious badge denoting the wearer eschewed alcohol) and the solicitor says to me, "You're for the high-jump now, wee man." I was frightened, you know. But I only got a month's suspended sentence.'

Far from learning his lesson, Paddy gleefully told himself he 'had gotten away with it', and it was not long before he returned to his hefty consumption of alcohol, driving home after a hard night's drinking and convincing himself that he 'wasn't too drunk'.

It was on his return from another long night in the shebeens, in early 1980, that he was caught drink-driving for a second time.

'It was a Sunday and we had started drinking at three o'clock in the afternoon until about two or three in the morning. And I thought I could drive alright, no problem. Up through Rathcoole housing estate was no bother, then I got to O'Neill Road roundabout near the graveyard and the next thing the sliding door opens. Then it fell off and the oul car conked out on me.'

Paddy stared at the car door lying on the road, the cool February night air breezing in through the fresh opening. He wondered how he was going to struggle out and fix it back on; there was no way he could lift it by himself. It soon ceased to be his most pressing problem. Through a drunken haze he watched as a member of the Royal Ulster Constabulary appeared. The officer was only too glad to put an end to Paddy's dilemma.

'So, the next thing I see is this policeman coming across the road towards me and he says, "Sir, I think you're drunk", and I says, "You better believe it!"'

With that Paddy was pulled out of the car and taken to the local police station and charged with driving while unfit. Meanwhile, unknown to Paddy, the security guards in their hut at Camco were tuned in to the police radio on their walkie-talkies, an illegal but common practice during the Troubles. They heard the whole exchange taking place.

Roaring with laughter, the security men soon spread the word about 'Paddy the delinquent'. Unaware that tales of his misdeed had been relayed across the shop floor, Paddy returned to work, the picture of innocence. His drunken indiscretion provided a source of banter and teasing for the next couple of weeks.

'There was a great laugh in work when I got in two days

later and they were able to tell me what happened word for word,' he says.

While his second run-in with the law provided no end of laughs at work, it was another story altogether when he appeared in front of the magistrate at Newtownabbey Court.

'Adams was the resident magistrate. He knew that I had a half bottle of vodka and a couple of beers in the three-wheeler when I was arrested. Adams says to me, "Now, if your barrister had told me that at that time of the morning you were very cold, Mr Grimshaw, and you had that in there to keep you warm I would have had no hesitation in throwing the case out. But seeing he didn't do that," he banged his gavel, "in you go. You're banned for two years." When Musgrave Police Station heard about this they took the car off me.'

It had been dawning on Paddy for some time that his drinking was spiralling out of control. When he wasn't working, he was out socialising and drinking; it came with the territory and Paddy had thrown himself into it wholeheartedly. He also saw it as a way of giving the two finger salute to those who had dictated how he lived his life in the past. He had revelled in his unruly ways but now things were unravelling around him. With no car his mobility was severely restricted and he was dependent on others for lifts to and from work — and to and from the pub. He now concedes that he had probably been an alcoholic for a long time before he was arrested for drink-driving.

'I was very, very foolish for at least ten years. You could say I was an alcoholic. I had to answer to nobody but myself. I had no matrons to tell me off like at the home in Bangor. I was saying to myself, "I'm free now; I can do what I like. I can smoke now." It was very much rebellion against the system. I was never told I was an alcoholic, I just assumed I was. I was drinking heavily to forget my past.'

His health eventually succumbed to his incessant drinking. One evening, shortly after leaving the Intercontinental Hotel in Belfast city centre, he collapsed in the street.

'Even though I wasn't singing or anything, I used to go to these clubs. I was walking along, just where the law courts are in the city centre, and I collapsed with exhaustion.'

He was rushed to the Royal Victoria Hospital on the Falls Road in west Belfast where doctors found that he had a collapsed lung. It should have been a timely warning but Paddy paid little heed and kept on drinking.

'The doctors said it was wear and tear of my body. I stopped drinking then but after a while I went back on the drink. I sort of thought, I'm young, I can do anything. I had lost the three-wheeler, but one will never learn. If I had my life to live over..." he says, his voice tinged with regret, leaving his sentence hanging.

In the months following Paddy's release from hospital, fate and the Troubles combined to force a dramatic change in his life. It took a bomb, literally under his backside, to shake him up and startle him into changing his ways. He was still living with Mr and Mrs Elliott opposite the Hatfield Bar on the Ormeau Road when the police were given a warning that a bomb had been planted at Martins' builders' yard, on the next row over from the Elliotts' house, at the bottom of University Avenue. While the police were busy evacuating the area, Paddy was in the bathroom on the top floor of the house having a nice, relaxing soak in the bath, completely oblivious to the panic on the streets two floors below him.

'It was a three-storey house and I was in the very top room. I was in the bath when I heard a big bang and the blooming bath lifted right off the floor. Lucky enough, there was only a small window in the bathroom and that came crashing in with the blast.'

Shaken and dazed, Paddy crawled out of the bathroom, grabbed a towel and scrambled downstairs to see what had happened.

'I was thin in those days and I was able to get down the stairs. There were police everywhere. One policeman caught sight of me coming out the front door and he says, "In the name of Jesus, what happened here?" I hadn't realised there had been a warning. I said, "I never heard you. I was up in the bath." There was nobody else in the house; Mr and Mrs Elliott were all out. He just shrugged his shoulders and laughed. A guy called Martin Sharpe told me afterwards that he was shouting at everyone to get out; there was a bomb ready to go off. I had a lucky escape.'

The bomb that blew Paddy out of his bath forced him to up sticks and move from the Ormeau Road. He had had enough of the Troubles which, in March 1981, were building in intensity with the emergence of the second set of hunger strikes by republican prisoners at the Maze Prison outside Lisburn.

It was time to move out of the city, which had become a prime location for loyalist and republican killings. Paddy heard from a couple of men at work that there was a spare room at their lodgings close to Ballyclare, about ten miles outside Belfast,

'I heard about it from the African guys in the electrical department in Camco. They were living with a Mrs Bradford and they were able to tell me that there was a vacant room in the lodgings because they were leaving. I rang her and she said to come over and see it. So I went up that night and I took it.'

Jenny Bradford and her husband Norman had a farmhouse on the Irish Hill Road near Ballyclare, where they lived with their son and daughter, who were in secondary education. Norman worked in the General Electric Company in Larne and, after work each day, when he came home, he put in some time on the farm. It was far removed from Paddy's former hunting grounds in the city but he was glad of the break. He still did the occasional gig with the Dollars in Larne but he gradually tired of travelling the country and traipsing in and out of the city.

'I must have sung for the best part of twenty years but I couldn't keep it up anymore. I gave it all up because I was basically fed up with it. Time was catching up with me. Then, when I moved up to Irish Hill Road, it was a different sort of life, out in the countryside. It was lonely out there but Mrs Bradford was a very good landlady. The lack of an invalid car affected my decision to give up the gigs because I had lost my licence. I had to get taxis to places and it was very expensive — £4, for instance, to get from the Irish Hill Road to Rathcoole.'

Paddy had enjoyed his singing days even though they came at a cost. He had lost his car, his freedom and his health.

'They were good days but very tiresome. I burned the candle at both ends. I had some stamina in the early days. I made the odd couple of friends even though I was never one for making friends. I just lived my own life, a loner. My disability did affect me. I was very shy, very backward — I wouldn't have said boo to a cow. The singing drew me out of myself and I was glad for it while it lasted.'

7

TWO WEEKS AFTER his arrival at Mrs Bradford's farmhouse, Paddy was rushed into hospital for emergency surgery. He had suffered a secondary appendix which was the result of residual infection from his original appendectomy when he was in Stewart Memorial as a child.

'I was rushed to Larne for the operation. It saved my life. An ex-RAF surgeon operated on me. The tubes were coming out of me everywhere — if I hadn't had the operation I would have died.'

After the operation Paddy spent a month recuperating in a convalescent home outside Larne. A month later he returned to work in Camco. But his health continued to deteriorate and, in the autumn of 1981, he was made redundant. After almost twenty years with the company he received a £2,500 redundancy package and a company pension.

For many, retiring to the countryside would be a dream come true but for Paddy, at thirty-seven, the tranquillity of rural County Antrim brought him little peace. The prospect of never working again was debilitating and frustrating. He had nothing outside his job. It was his life. Since he had all but given up on the singing circuit he'd lost contact with most of his friends in the bars. He became very depressed and turned to drink to assuage his bouts of melancholy. With few friends, apart from his landlady Mrs Bradford, and the lodgers who came and went, he threw himself into drinking as a distraction. He passed the days by spending what little mobility allowance he received by ferrying in and out to the pubs in Ballyclare.

'I was just basically idle. I wasn't working. I had nobody to turn to help me get back to work so I started getting heavy into the drink. I got very down; only for the other lodgers, I would have cracked up. I wouldn't have stayed very long. But then I had nowhere else to go. It was very difficult to get your day in. They were very long old days. I had no transport because I had lost my last invalid car and had nothing to do. When I had to get my money from Ballyclare, I got the school bus in the morning and then, in the afternoon, I sneaked into the bars to blow it all. I never took drink up to the house. I always got taxis back and forwards into Ballyclare and drank in the pubs there.'

While a drink was important to Paddy, he was a force to be reckoned with if he didn't get a smoke.

'There was a wee shop, Rankins, on the Hillhead Road. I got to know the woman in it very well and, if I was short of cash, until I got my dole money the next week, then she would have given me my fags.'

Mrs Bradford took great care of Paddy as he was a permanent lodger and he felt very comfortable in her home and with her family. He had his own room upstairs and there were five other bedrooms for the lodgers who passed through. He grew very fond of Mrs Bradford over the years and her unquestioning hospitality.

'She was your typical country woman, a very kind person. She would never see you stuck. She was very, very good to me,' he recalls. 'I had my own room and then their big Hunter Reeves fire in the kitchen. She was a good cook and I was well looked after, although the winters were long. She had no central heating in the place and up in my bedroom I just had a gas fire.'

Seventy-five-year-old Mrs Bradford recalls that she was very fond of 'Pat' herself and treated him like one of the family.

'I suppose with him going from house to house this was the only home he ever knew. He never knew what people were like, living in a home environment together. In the places he was before he would have got his meals but he wouldn't have been mixing with the people in the same way, whereas with us, he was one of the family and that was just it.

'We never made any differences with anybody: if you had to wash a dish, then if you were able, you washed it; if you wanted a cup of tea, then you could make it. Pat told us all about his homes from the day he was born right through. He just accepted it.'

There were many lodgers at Mrs Bradford's and Paddy was kept busy with the constant flow of people through the farmhouse.

'There were plenty of foreigners over the years: Germans, Americans, Swiss, and Canadians.'

Indeed, Mrs Bradford says Paddy was never stuck for someone to chat to.

'We had so many people in all the time and Paddy was able to talk to them. He was a very friendly person, he could get on with everybody and talk to everybody — it didn't matter who you were. I always said that Pat must have had had some sort of status in his genes. He was one of those types of people who got on well with everybody. With the lodgers coming and going we had a full house and he always enjoyed the banter with them.'

Away from the banter and joking Paddy shared with Mrs Bradford and his surrogate family, he silently mourned for the family he had never had. He often wondered if his own family gathered about their dinner table laughing and joking as he did with Mrs Bradford's family. With too much time on his hands as an unemployed man, Paddy began to dwell very heavily on his missing relatives. Mrs Bradford had invited him along to the Loo church in Ballyclare and it was here he confided in the minister, Reverend John Nelson, about his circumstances and his desire to find out who his parents were, and more particularly, his desire to seek out his mother. Reverend Nelson decided to assist Paddy in his task. On 21 June 1982 he took Paddy to the General Records Office in Belfast's Chichester Street, where birth, marriage and death certificates are held. It was here that Paddy laid eyes on his own birth certificate for the first time.

He remembers how much it cost to purchase a copy of the certificate which gave the information he had spent his whole life wondering about — who his mother was. After thirty-eight years the price of this knowledge came at the paltry sum of £3.50.

'I had never seen my birth certificate until then. I was always told that I wasn't legally entitled to my birth certificate. In those days people who were adopted had no right to see the original birth certificate with their parents' names on it.'

The Reverend Nelson was also astute enough to request Paddy's parents' marriage certificate which listed their addresses at the time, and the names of the couple's fathers.

Suddenly, before Paddy's eyes, lay the name of his mother and the name and address of his father. He was filled with a mixture of elation and sadness. This transformed his mother into a real person. He now had a name that he could start to build a face around — Philomena. There was also an address in west Belfast where she lived with her father — his grandfather — James.

With his hopes rising, an inner voice was shouting, 'I have a family'; at the same time his heart was cautioning him not to get carried away. Certificates in hand, Reverend Nelson took Paddy to the Public Records Office of Northern Ireland on Balmoral Avenue in south Belfast to try to find further information about his parents. They found nothing. Paddy had no idea where to begin to search and Reverend Nelson had done all he could think of. In just one day, Paddy felt that he had found his family and lost them again. He was heartbroken; he had his mother's name and an image of her forming in his mind but she had vanished again in front of his very eyes.

In the weeks that followed Paddy became depressed, a fact he kept well hidden from Mrs Bradford, fooling her with his usual barrage of banter. He again turned to alcohol in a bid to cope with the renewed feelings of abandonment that had surfaced to torture him again. He gradually became enslaved to the ritual of spending his incapacity benefit and income support money on drink, leaving little for anything else. Mrs Bradford failed to notice Paddy's depression.

Indeed, she says he wasn't the type to get depressed — he 'just got on with things'. But she does recall that Paddy spent a lot of time and money on alcohol.

'Pat was heavy into the drink. God, it was terrible. He blew hundreds and hundreds of pounds on drink,' she says.

His drinking continued until Paddy found himself in severe financial difficulties with no apparent means of escape. Then one day he was out on his regular Friday night shopping trip with Mrs Bradford and her husband at the Abbey Centre in Newtownabbey when he bumped into an old friend, William Auld. William had been one of Paddy's few friends at Stewart Memorial Home but the pair hadn't seen each other since their early twenties when Paddy was a member of the Polio Fellowship. As they reminisced Paddy confessed to William that he was badly in debt and desperately needed money to cover his keep in Mrs Bradford's bed and breakfast. Mrs Bradford had been very patient with him and had turned a blind eye to the mounting debt Paddy owed her, because he was a good tenant. But Paddy felt uneasy at abusing her kindness. He had applied for a £500 loan from the credit union in Ballyclare but, since he hadn't contributed much in the way of savings over the years, it was refused. William said he would have a word with the Polio Fellowship committee and get back to him. Paddy hadn't been a member of the Fellowship for years and didn't expect any financial aid to be approved by the committee. It wasn't, but the request did open the door for Paddy to return to the Fellowship. Unfortunately, by this stage, Paddy was well immersed in his alcoholic lifestyle and had no interest in what he viewed as a swarm of busy-bodies prying into his life. He was doing just fine without them. Drinking had become his main occupation and this had made him a little twisted towards the people he had once thought fondly of. Nevertheless, William set about a plan to coax Paddy back into the fold.

'William must have talked to Jean Thompson in the Polio Fellowship and she rang me. I was still drinking at that stage and I said I didn't want to be anywhere near the Fellowship.'

Ms Thompson was a persistent woman and hammered away at Paddy to return and, after much badgering, he eventually gave in.

The Polio Fellowship had been in decline for a number of years and Ms Thompson was delighted to have Paddy, one of its original members, back. While Paddy was renewing acquaintances with old friends, Norman Bradford's health was failing and Mrs Bradford decided that closing the bed and breakfast to look after him was the best thing to do. For fourteen years her farmhouse had been home to Paddy. She knew he would need time to find a new place, so she took him into her confidence.

'My husband was ill and I had to look after him, and I was getting tired running the bed and breakfast. Well, it happened to be that there was a postman who came to the house and his sister was something to do with a development called Chisholm Court in Ballyclare, and they had these flats that were being finished off, so he told Pat about them. Inside two months Pat had the keys for the flat. It was one of these things that were meant to be.'

Paddy's own health had been deteriorating down the years, assisted by his considerable alcohol consumption and sparse activity. He had transformed from his once agile, svelte figure into a stocky build of a man, unsure on his feet.

'I was never as glad to see anyone in a flat. When he was here he was as skinny as you could have got them,' Mrs Bradford says with a chuckle. 'He was out with the bands and singing. But as the years went by and he stopped working and singing he couldn't get about as well. He had only left here a couple of months when he came up to the house to visit and he couldn't get up the stairs.'

In June 1994, Paddy moved into Chisholm Court fold, a two-minute walk from the town square, on the Doagh Road in Ballyclare. Paddy celebrated his fiftieth birthday there just three months after moving into his self-contained flat. Glasses were raised to toast his health but there was no alcohol for Paddy. Six months before his move to Chisholm Court he had been diagnosed with diabetes and told that he needed to stop drinking immediately. Paddy heeded his doctor's advice and ended a drinking spree that had spanned almost three and a half decades.

In 1996, after two years in his new home, Paddy was reunited with his good friend Eddie McCrory. It had been almost twenty years since the pair had last seen each other and it was quite a shock to Eddie when they finally came face to face.

'I lost contact with Paddy when I drifted away from the Polio Fellowship,' Eddie says. 'It was only when I came back to an AGM dinner that I saw him again. I nearly died of shock. When I knew him he was thin and then the next time I saw him he was the size of a house. I didn't see the in between bit. This fellow came over and it was the voice — he said, "You don't recognise me." I said, "I don't recognise you but I know the voice. You're Paddy Grimshaw. If you'd walked by me I wouldn't have known who you were till you opened your mouth."'

Eddie continues: 'I would not have recognised Paddy, ever. He was on two walking sticks and very, very slow. When I knew Paddy he was much more agile than me. He had long hair when I saw him last but at the dinner his hair was cropped tight to his head. He used to have it all combed over to the side.'

Once Eddie had recovered from the shock of Paddy's striking transformation, the pair spent time catching up on the last twenty years. In the intervening period Eddie had married and he and his wife Susan had three children. Paddy had no wife to tell of but he did confide in Eddie about his burning desire to find his mother.

8

FIVE YEARS AFTER Paddy and Eddie were reunited, Paddy made one of the most important decisions of his life — to begin the search for his mother. He had mentioned to Eddie many times before that he wanted to find her but, in the summer of 2001, he finally took the steps to attempt to make it a reality. He wasn't optimistic about finding her by himself but he felt sure that, if anyone could help, Eddie could.

'Paddy had always said to me that he wanted to find his mother. He said he never had any animosity towards her. He just said he would love to find her. He presumed she was in Milltown, the Catholic cemetery in Belfast. He wanted to go to her grave and tell her that he bore her no grudge,' Eddie says. 'Then at the Polio Fellowship annual meeting about five years ago, Paddy handed me this brown envelope and said, "That's those things I said I would get you."'

Eddie didn't open the envelope immediately but waited until he arrived home later that afternoon. When he looked at its contents he had a pleasant surprise. The envelope held Paddy's birth certificate and his mother's marriage certificate.

'When I saw Tommy Grimshaw's address — Woodstock Street — I recognised it as one of the streets in the Short Strand area where I came from.'

Eddie knew instantly that he would be able to find somebody who knew the Grimshaw family.

'I knew people who lived on Woodstock Street originally. I knew one Grimshaw from the credit union from years before who had gone to live somewhere else. I remember once asking this guy if he had any relatives who had polio — it was such an unusual name — but he said he didn't. When I saw the address, I phoned Paddy straight away and asked him if he was absolutely sure he really wanted me to trace these people because I might be able to do something.'

Paddy was shocked that Eddie had been able to find a lead so quickly. A little unnerved, he had mixed feelings, but he had come this far, so was determined to go through with it and see what they could find. He told Eddie to go ahead.

'I was taken aback, I didn't think we would have got anywhere and certainly not so quickly,' he says. 'I was kind of apprehensive and then I thought, he has gone to all that trouble, we may as well go on. Actually, I was not confident that anything would come out of it all but Eddie is a determined man.'

Eddie began making phone calls. As an officer in the local credit union, he was well known in the area and knew most of the residents. He also knew exactly the woman to phone to inquire about Tommy Grimshaw.

'This woman had lived in Woodstock Street. She said she had known the Grimshaws. She recalled a Tommy

Grimshaw who had a son, Joe, who now lived in Twinbrook. She didn't think there were any other children. She said couldn't remember what happened to the wife but that Tommy went to live in England.'

The woman put Eddie in contact with another lady from the Short Strand, Nellie Fagan, who had known some of the Grimshaw family.

'So I went to Nellie's house and I asked her, "Would you know somebody called Joe Grimshaw?" and she says, "Aye, sure, he works over in the bus depot."' The Translink bus depot was just yards from the Fagan household.

Now hot on the trail, Eddie believed he may have stumbled upon a relative of Paddy's, perhaps a cousin or a more distant relation. He then approached his brother-in-law, Will Baker, who worked as a bus inspector and who was based in the Short Strand Translink depot. Will did know a Joe Grimshaw who worked as a mechanic at the depot. He told Eddie he thought Joe was an only child. Will offered to take the documents and show them to Joe.

Eddie takes up the story once more: 'Joe was in a pit working on the underside of a bus and came up to speak to my brother-in-law. Will explained about the man from the Polio Fellowship who was trying to trace his family and that we thought he may have some family connection with Joe. Will handed the birth certificate and marriage certificate to the mechanic.'

After wiping hands, Joe looked first at the wedding document. He was surprised to see the legal details of his parents' marriage.

Eddie recalls: 'Joe says, "That's my mammy and daddy's certificate", and Will says, "Well, that's Paddy's mother and father." The fella nearly fell into the pit!'

Paddy initially didn't believe Eddie when he rang to say that he had found his brother. It had, after all, only been a week since Paddy gave him the documents to start the search.

'He rang to say, "I think we have found a brother in the Strand Bus Depot." I thought he was only joking but he says, "Do you want to meet him?"'

After the initial shock, Paddy was eager to meet Joe. He couldn't believe he actually had a brother and needed to see him to make it real. Completely unnerved by the discovery, he ensured that Eddie would be by his side for the meeting.

Eddie arranged for the brothers to get together at his own house. He picked Paddy up from Ballyclare and brought him to his home in Carryduff on the outskirts of south Belfast. At the same time, Eddie arranged for his niece to collect Joe Grimshaw and his wife and bring them to Carryduff. It was a stressful situation for all concerned. Eddie recalls Paddy saying to him before Joe and his wife arrived, "Right, we'll play this cool. Just wait and see. We'll not get too excited."

'But,' Eddie says, 'the minute Joe came through the door, instead of playing cool, Paddy couldn't restrain himself and immediately thrust the marriage and birth documents at him.'

'I was very nervous,' Paddy says by way of explanation. 'The night was okay but it was very nerve-wracking. Everybody was uptight. When I say uptight, I mean meeting somebody for the first time — it wasn't easy, it wasn't easy at all.'

9

FAIR-HAIRED, GREEN-EYED Joseph Grimshaw was born in 1941 into a world in turmoil. The Second World War was in full flow. Earlier that year, Belfast, a city previously untouched by the ravages of war, was attacked by German bombers. Newly-married Philomena Grimshaw was three months pregnant with her son at the time and living with her husband Tommy above a shop in the Short Strand area of east Belfast.

Eighteen-year-old Philomena had been born on 5 October 1922 to James and Sarah Murray of Majorca Street in west Belfast. She married Thomas Grimshaw who, born on 15 February 1918, was four years her senior. He was the son of Mary and William Grimshaw, from Woodstock Street, in the Short Strand. The couple were married at St Paul's Church on the Falls Road on 10 September 1940. There had been few guests in attendance but Philomena's father, a lamp-lighter by trade, gave his young daughter away to her twenty-two-year-old sweetheart. Tommy's parents, on the other hand, were not in attendance; indeed, they were not even aware the marriage was taking place and when they found out they were not happy. Even so, after the couple's wedding, Tommy and Philomena moved to an address just a few doors away from his parents' house.

With its reputation for technical ingenuity, and a vast pool of skilled labour, Belfast was, in 1936, a major centre for aircraft production. The Belfast Harbour Commissioners obtained permission from the British parliament to build a large aerodrome at Sydenham, just a stone's throw from the Short Strand. Short Brothers were then persuaded, with the help of government financing, to join Harland & Wolff in building an aircraft factory at Queen's Island on the banks of the River Lagan, leading to the docks and Belfast Lough. The factory was less than three miles from Philomena's new marital home. The government believed that locating a weapons production factory in Belfast would be far enough removed from the rest of Britain to avoid attack from the Germans. They were wrong.

They had failed to adequately assess the danger to the city's residents or the capabilities of the Luftwaffe bombers. Blackout procedures across Belfast were sloppy at best and many historians point to the apathy of the people in the city, who resented having to obey 'cocky air raid wardens'. People were convinced, as was the government, that Belfast would not be attacked. That apathy lasted only until the terrifying early hours of 15 April 1941 when German bombs began to rain down on the city. The Luftwaffe, reportedly mistaking the small lakes of the Waterworks, a north Belfast beauty spot, for the River Lagan, concentrated their offensive on that packed residential area. One bomb dropped on the corner of Oxford Street and East Bridge

Street in the city centre, wiping out the city's telephone service and leaving Belfast without communication. York Street spinning factory, the largest of its kind in Europe, was destroyed and more than thirty people were killed. As the 'all-clear' sounded at 5am on 16 April the death toll was more than 700 and counting, with 1,500 injured and more than 1,600 houses damaged beyond repair. A little over a month later, on 4 May, the city was barely recovering when it was attacked again. This time the Luftwaffe had none of the difficulties of their first raid. They struck at the very heart of Belfast's industry — the shipyards. Almost half of all shipbuilding construction was lost. This time 150 people were killed. In response to the onslaught, more than 49,000 people were evacuated from the city.

The blitz was a massive blow to people of the city as already shaky employment levels dropped to lows similar to those of the Depression, which had ended a few years earlier. The war had become a reality for the citizens of Belfast. With the real prospect of being bombed again and food rationing in place, it was not a joyous world to be bringing a child into. But Joseph Grimshaw was on his way and, on 25 September 1941, Philomena presented her husband with a baby son at the Jubilee Maternity Hospital — formerly part of the City Hospital — on the Lisburn Road.

Joseph, or Joe as he prefers, doesn't remember his mother. She left him and her husband in 1943 when he was only two years old. After her departure Joe was raised by his grandparents, Mary and William, on the same street that his parents had shared their brief marriage. The brevity of the union was of little surprise to his grandparents given the couple's hasty and clandestine wedding but this was a view they kept from their grandson for some time.

During the remaining years of the war, Joe and his grandparents were evacuated from the city along with thousands of others citizens.

'I went to live in a place called Mayobridge outside Newry in County Down during the war,' Joe says. 'Most children were evacuated at that age. I was down there for about two years. I came back here with my grandparents when they thought the war was over and lived with them in Woodstock Street. I attended St Anthony's Primary School, about a mile away on the Woodstock Road.'

Joe did not know any family other than his grandparents, his father and his uncle James. So, when they told him that his mother was their daughter, and she had died a month after he was born, he had no reason to believe otherwise.

'My grandparents said my mother was a woman named Molly and I believed them. Their daughter died from meningitis a month after I was born and I was always told that she was my mother. It didn't make any difference to me. To me, they were my parents. They were there for me and that was it.'

For years Joe grew up believing this tale. His father, Tommy, was a regular visitor to his grandparent's house and Joe knew that he was his dad but, in his young mind, there was nothing disjointed about that. The fact that that would make his father and mother brother and sister did not occur to him.

In 1948 work was thin on the ground in Belfast and Tommy Grimshaw moved to Scotland in search of a new job and a new life. Joe was seven years of age when his father left him with his grandparents.

'My father had worked in Inglis's Bakery in the Markets area and then he worked in the shipyard. When work became kind of slack he decided to go to Scotland where he got a job in the coal mines, where he worked for years.'

Joe was not overly upset by his father's departure; he had been in and out of his life over the years but it was his grandparents whom Joe thought of as his real parents, and on whom he relied.

Tommy was a thirty-year-old man with an estranged wife and a seven-year-old son; he was still young and his parents encouraged him to get out and take a second stab at his life. Joe was in safe hands with them, they told him. With his father's assurances that he would be back to visit him, Joe went about his young life without a worry. It was not until a few months after his father's move that a peculiar encounter on the street near his grandparents' house triggered off some curious questions about his family.

'I was about seven or eight and I was playing football around the streets and somebody shouted "Joe" to me — one of my mates, I thought — and I said, "What do you want?" Then somebody else shouted "Joe" and I turned around and it was a woman.

'She says, "Joe?" and I said, "Yeah." And she says, "Do they call you Joe Grimshaw?" and I says, "Yes" and she says, "I'm your mother."'

Joe was confused and a little angry. He looked her up and down incredulously, taking in her polished snakeskin shoes and matching handbag, and then told her that she was not his mummy.

'I says, "You're not my mummy. My mummy's Molly." I just looked at her. I can't remember her face too much but what I do remember is that the snakeskin shoes looked funny to me. She just stood back and said again, "I am your mother" and I said, "No, you're not, my mummy's Molly", and I ran away.'

Joe hurried to his grandparents' house to tell them about the woman but when they came out to find her she was gone. Joe was upset by the drama but his grandparents assured him that his mummy, Molly, was dead and he gradually forgot about the stranger. He brushed off the experience but over the next few years it came back to play on his mind. He began ruminating on what the woman had said and eventually came to the conclusion that something just wasn't right.

'When I had a bit of sense I heard them talking about Molly and I said to myself, "How could Molly be my mother if she is my father's sister?" I thought about this and I queried it and my granny just happened to say, "No, your mother and father broke up when you were about two years old and went their separate ways."'

Nine-year-old Joe was too young to understand or question why his mother had left and it didn't bother him unduly. His grandmother was the only mother he had ever known; he had a dad and a granddad, and he didn't know any different.

'They were my parents to me,' he says simply. 'I thought maybe my grandparents were trying to save me embarrassment about my mother and father being separated.'

Joe let it rest. He had no memory of his mother, and his grandmother and grandfather had filled the gap in his life that she had created, so he never felt loss from her absence. Again they had cushioned him against the coarse realities of life. However, four years after the woman's visit, Joe received another shock — this time right on his doorstep.

'Years later, I got a letter with my name on it. It was marked "Private and Confidential". It said, "I'm your mother and I want to see you at the summer house in Hickeyman's Park."'

The 'park' was a tiny triangular piece of ground on the River Lagan bounded by the Albert Bridge and the Ravenhill Road.

'I was wondering what was going on,' Joe says, 'so I showed the letter to my grandmother and she looked at it but she didn't say anything. She called my uncle in — my father's older brother, James — and he looked at it. He says, "Right, I'll deal with this." I think it might have been a day or two later when I was supposed to see her; he went up towards the park and he came back half an hour later and said there was nobody there. James said he thought the woman may have spotted him and made herself scarce.

'I was uneasy about it. I thought maybe I should have said nothing — she couldn't have kidnapped me or anything. But I was wondering why she was wanting to contact me — that was twice you know. I was about eleven years of age the second time. After that there was no more contact.'

Joe says he attempted to force thoughts of his runaway mother out of his head.

'I forgot about it. I just sort of blanked it out because once they said she wasn't there — if she was my mother, then she would have been there, or she would have come looking for me. When I thought about it years later, I thought maybe I should have gone and saw the woman. Then I asked myself why she left my da. I didn't know what the score was.'

Joe heard no more from his mother after her last attempt

to contact him and from his grandparents' tone he gathered that it was not up for discussion. He does, however, have a vague recollection of going to visit a woman whom his granny later told him was his other grandmother.

'They lived in Joy Street in the Markets, just across the Albert Bridge from the Short Strand. I remember visiting once with my grandparents, vaguely. There was no grandfather there — I presumed he was dead,' he says.

There was no further mention of his mother until a few years later. Joe recalls having to go with his grandmother to serve divorce papers to his mother on his father's behalf.

'My father sent the divorce papers. I had a wee form and on it were the words, "Divorce papers to be served on Philomena Grimshaw." The house was in Wells Street. That was off the Woodstock Road. I remember me and my grandmother walking up to it and we knocked on the door and the people told us they had never heard of her. And I just put it back in the envelope and that was the last I ever heard her being mentioned. After so many years, the marriage became annulled, so eventually he was able to get married in Scotland.'

Joe didn't want to ask his father about his mother, especially after his remarriage, so it was never talked about.

'I didn't want to bring it up. He had remarried again and had three girls who are half-sisters to me. He came back and forth to visit me twice a year in my grandmother's house. He actually brought one of the girls over with his wife.'

In his late teens Joe again began to wonder what had happened between his mother and father. When he was eighteen his grandparents decided to tell him what little they said they knew.

'They got married too young,' Joe says. 'He was twenty-two and she was nineteen on her next birthday. My grandparents didn't take to that — he was too young. He hadn't told them he was getting married; he just went ahead and did it. She was what they called a "night-time girl", who loved going to dances and socialising, whereas my father was on shift work. He wanted to see that I was brought up right. So they must have had some sort of a row. All my grandparents said was that there was a child born but it was years after they separated. I didn't know anything about P J and it never entered my head to think about it. I had no interest in anything like that at that age.'

Joe's grandparents died when he was twenty-two. He was distraught.

'When they died my world collapsed,' he says. 'But that's life — it has to go on.'

He had kept in touch with his father but, after his grandparents' deaths, Tommy's visits became less frequent until eventually they rarely saw each other. Then one day, when Joe's father was in his early fifties, he rang Joe out of the blue and asked him to try to find his mother. Joe believes he was trying to put old ghosts to rest.

'He wanted to find out himself whether she was alive or dead. I tried to go through records at a place in Chichester Street. I asked them if they would go through the records and try to find Philomena Grimshaw or Murray. After about three weeks there was still no trace so I let it go at that and I wrote back to my father and told him there was no answer. He dropped it after that.'

He and his father kept in contact through telephone calls and sporadic visits but, after Joe's marriage in 1973, they lost touch again. Two years later, Joe decided to try to re-establish contact.

'I lost contact with him because he had moved from Scotland to Luton where he worked in Vauxhall's motor company. I got a couple I knew to enquire about him and they said, yes, he worked in Vauxhall's and they knew a Thomas Grimshaw. So I got them to talk to him. I got a phone call and I recognised the voice. That was 1975.'

Three months later Joe made his way over to Luton to visit his father who was now aged fifty-seven. But the father and son hadn't seen each other in more than a decade and it did not occur to them how time might have changed their appearances.

'Me and the wife went, and I'm looking for a guy with black wavy hair and he's looking for a wee skinny guy. I made my way off the bus and he's coming towards me and I'm walking that way and we walk by each other. I look and say, "Nah, that man's not black-haired," and he stops and he looks at me and he says, "Joe?" It was about eleven years since I had seen him. I stayed for about three weeks in his house.

'I kept in contact for a long time after that. He was going to come over and visit me but he fell and tore ligaments in his leg and that was that scrubbed.'

Joe and Tommy never saw each other in person again, but were in contact by letter and by telephone until Tommy's death in August 1995. He'd suffered a stroke from which he was gradually recovering.

'I kept in contact right up until he died, but he couldn't talk on the phone because he had lost the power of speech with the stroke, so he did a bit of scribbling but gradually it stopped. Then he took another mini-stroke and he gave instructions that if he didn't improve, the life-support system was to be switched off. Then he took pneumonia and I got a phone call from his oldest girl to tell me that he had passed away during the night. He was seventy-seven. That was it, a chapter closed,' Joe says with a sigh.

After his father's death, the only immediate family Joe had was his wife, Ann, and their two daughters, Claire and Joanne. As an employee of Translink in Belfast he was working towards retirement and enjoying getting to know his two grandchildren at his home in Twinbrook. When Will Baker approached him in the Short Strand bus depot on that summer afternoon in 2001, sixty-year-old Joe was far from prepared for what he was about to hear. He said he was caught completely unawares.

'Will came in and said he had something to tell me. He said he knew a man called Grimshaw and that he knew it wasn't a very common name. But when he said P J Grimshaw, he was talking to a blank wall. I didn't know what he was talking about. It stunned me and I said, "I can't think who this guy is." It was a big, big shock. Here I am, all these years believing that I am an only son; out of the blue you get that and it explodes your head.'

But Will had his mother and father's marriage certificate and, on Paddy's birth certificate, Tommy Grimshaw was listed as Paddy's father. It was baffling.

'I didn't get too upset. I thought there was something funny going on here. My father had never mentioned anything to me about another family, because he would have. He didn't keep quiet about the three girls he had in England,' Joe says.

The meeting with Paddy, he says, was a strange occasion. It all happened so fast. Two weeks after he learned he had a brother, he was going to meet him. Stranger still was the fact that he had known Paddy's friend, Eddie, from many years ago while growing up in the Short Strand. So when he met

Paddy in Eddie's house that August evening, it was quite a surreal experience.

'I hadn't seen Eddie for years but I remembered his ginger hair. I remember him going to St Matthew's Church, and I used to see him walking up the aisle to Communion.'

Eddie also knew Joe from the credit union in the Short Strand where he has carried out voluntary work since the 1970s.

'Joe came into the credit union regularly and I had often meant to ask him if he knew Paddy but I never got around to it,' Eddie says.

Joe says his meeting with Paddy was an uncomfortable one. He was taken aback to see his brother in a wheelchair. He had no idea that Paddy had polio.

'I met him in Eddie's house and sat and talked to him. I felt so sorry when I saw him — the way he was — but I didn't let him see that. I didn't expect to see him in a wheelchair; I wasn't told this. I tried to see if there was any resemblance but my wife told me she didn't see any resemblance.'

From all accounts, there was a definite air of tension present during the meeting. From their conversation Joe could tell that Paddy was at pains to discover if they did indeed share the same father. Joe's instinct was that they did not.

'I think P J was trying to figure out if my father was his father. My gut feeling was that he was not. My father would have said something during the years that I knew him. No one ever told me that I had any brothers or sisters, so I grew up with the feeling that I was an only son. The years between me and P J would be significant for P J to think that my father was his father, because my parents separated after two years and that would be 1943, and Paddy was born in

1944. I don't think my father knew anything. If he did, he never said to me. That's my gut feeling. It's not that I wanted it that way. It doesn't matter now. My father's name is on the birth certificate but my father would have told me these things and he never mentioned anyone.'

He also believes that his grandparents would have told him if they knew they had another grandchild. They wouldn't have ignored Paddy's existence.

'If my granny had known, she would have told me. She did say to me once that Philomena had a baby to another man and that they lived in Bangor about twelve miles from Belfast. That was all I knew. When I saw P J, I said to myself, "I wonder, is this the guy?"'

Joe's guess was correct: Paddy was that baby. Joe says he found the meeting very taxing. It was difficult to know what to say to Paddy. He felt for him but he couldn't help him find his mother, which was the one thing Paddy wanted to do. Joe had long ago put aside any thoughts of finding her. It was unfortunate for him to say so, given Paddy's circumstances, but he had been lucky enough in his life not to be greatly affected by Philomena's absence.

'It's hard to talk to people who you haven't been reared with. If you grew up with them or socialised with them you would be able to handle it better. I didn't even know my parents had married in St Paul's Church on the other side of town. P J had more gall to find out about it. It didn't bother me. My grandparents were like parents to me, so I had no reason to look for other family.'

Joe and Paddy parted after a long, difficult night of filling in the gaps in their respective lives. Joe left with a new half-brother and a commitment to stay in contact. When Eddie drove Paddy home to his flat in a sheltered fold dwelling in

Ballyclare that night, Joe decided to go along to see where Paddy lived. The night provided one other little incident which made an impact on Joe. When they arrived at the fold, Joe got out of the car to help Paddy into his apartment. As they reached the main door, Paddy realised he had forgotten his key and had to buzz for the warden to come out to let him in. Eddie recalls that Paddy's introduction of Joe to the warden left Joe stunned.

'Paddy said to the warden, "Have you met my brother, Joe?" as if they met quite regularly,' Eddie says. 'Joe came out shell-shocked at how easily Paddy just accepted it. He couldn't understand how easily he slipped into it.'

While Joe hadn't thought of his mother's whereabouts for years, his meeting with Paddy started him thinking again about what had happened to her. In 2005, four years after his first meeting with Paddy, Joe met a woman in a social club in the city centre who was about his mother's age. This encounter stirred some unsettling thoughts for Joe, provoking questions he might never find the answers to.

'It actually started with me asking older people at the club if they knew anyone from Joy Street in the Markets area. I knew these people came from that district and that was where my mother had lived. One woman said she had a friend coming home from the United States and she would bring her to the club and, if I wanted to talk to her, she would talk to me.

'I left that night and I forgot about the conservation but the woman from the United States did come over to me a couple of months ago and she said that my father had gotten a raw deal. I asked her why and she said, "She wasn't the woman for him." She didn't elaborate any more. She went back to America and I haven't seen her since.'

The exchange did nothing to resolve Joe's conflicting thoughts about his mother. Obviously the woman knew something about why his mother and father had separated but she wasn't willing to tell him. This served only to irk Joe. He is now vexed by the cryptic words of a woman who left him with more questions about the woman who bore his mother's name. 'I could never figure out why that woman said my father had a raw deal.'

Paddy's discovery of his new brother opened up a Pandora's box in Joe's life. In many ways Joe, who was happily preparing for a new life in retirement before his half-brother found him, wishes his life had not been disturbed. Old ghosts came back to haunt him, teasing him with their questions, the answers to which may already be secrets of the grave. Unfortunately for Joe, discovering that Paddy was his brother was not the last surprise fate had in store for him.

10

ALMOST EXACTLY A year after his detective work paid off with the discovery of Joe, Eddie received a phone call from an adoption agency in Belfast. They had a client looking for a Paddy Grimshaw. Through the telephone conversation, in the summer of 2002, it transpired that the agency had originally written to Joe, who had passed the letter on to Paddy. After ringing the agency, Paddy, perhaps feeling a little out of his depth, turned the situation over to his faithful friend Eddie to deal with.

'Luckily enough,' Eddie says, 'Joe had, by this time, met Paddy. If it had been the year before, then he wouldn't have known anything about all this.'

The adoption agency told Eddie they had been employed by the son of man in England who was looking for his brother, whom he knew to have polio and who had been put into care as a child. When Eddie confirmed that Paddy's identity matched that of the man they were looking for, the agency told him that their client's father was very keen to meet Paddy. Understandably, the news was quite a shock to Paddy.

'I was completely gobsmacked but happy at the same time. To have found one brother and then another in the space of a year, I was ecstatic.'

Gerard Campbell had known about his brother Paddy for almost forty years. On Halloween night in 1945, he'd been born to Philomena Grimshaw at the Jubilee Maternity Hospital in south Belfast. He was immediately given up for adoption.

On his birth certificate, where his father's name should have been, it simply stated 'unknown'. Gerard was taken to Nazareth Lodge Orphanage on the Ravenhill Road, where he spent the first years of his life. Four years later, he was adopted by Peter and Bridget Campbell from Newry. They had two children of their own, a fourteen-year-old daughter called Patsy and a twelve-year-old son named Jack.

Gerard says, 'Initially I was under supervision by the welfare department while I lived with the family and I grew up with the name Grimshaw. Then they adopted me properly and I assumed the family name, Campbell.'

Gerard's adoptive mother was forty-eight when she and her husband took Gerard into their home.

'Actually they didn't adopt me,' Gerard corrects himself with a laugh. 'It was my sister, Patsy, who decided. The family came down to Belfast looking for a little girl, she was looking for a sister, and they saw me and she liked the look of me. They took me out to the zoo a couple of times. Then they came and took me home with them.'

A skinny rake of a teenager with jet black hair and green eyes, Gerard was doted on by his new family. He had a very good upbringing and had 'no problems or hang-ups'.

Twelve years after he gave up the name Grimshaw, his welfare officer called to see him with some shocking news. Now fifteen years of age, he was completely unprepared for the jolt he was to receive that spring day in 1961. His welfare officer told him that he had an older brother called Patrick who was living in a boys' home in Belfast. Gerard was stunned. He never thought for a moment that he had any relatives outside his adoptive family and, suddenly, he was hit with the news that he had a brother. He had grown up all these years without ever knowing of his existence. He wondered if his brother knew about him. He decided he was going to go and find out.

'I was very curious and obviously a bit bewildered but I wanted to see him,' he says.

Gerard's parents were very supportive and encouraged him to find Paddy if that was what he wanted. It was. And with the help of his welfare officer, Gerard discovered the name of the home where Paddy was living and spoke to a clergyman there. The home was the Boys' Residential Home on Blacks Road.

'I found out that a guy who was supposed to be my brother was living in a hostel in Dunmurry run by a local church,' he says. 'I got the number and I rang this place and the guy said, "Yeah, there is a Patrick Grimshaw who lives here." I explained to him who I was and could I come and see him and he said, "Yeah." So I made arrangements to come down on the train. In those days I had to go into Belfast and then get a bus out to Dunmurry. So eventually I ended up at this hostel. When I got there this reverend said that Paddy was due in from work at about 5.15pm or 5.30pm.'

Gerard waited for over an hour but when Paddy did

arrive in from work he told the reverend he didn't want to see anybody.

'He was told that I was in the waiting room waiting for him and he wouldn't see me,' Gerard says, recalling his frustration. 'I was a bit disappointed and I left. I hadn't seen him at all.'

Gerard returned to Newry, disheartened and confused. He couldn't understand why his brother, his own flesh and blood, wouldn't want to see him. Refusing to accept defeat, he tried once more a few months later but with the same result.

'I got the feeling that this guy doesn't want to see me and I left it then. That was me finished with it then really.'

Two years later, in 1963, Gerard was serving time in a borstal in County Down for robbery when he received a very unexpected visitor.

'I was in Millisle doing some work for Her Majesty, as one does,' he laughs. 'I had actually robbed a small store. It was about three o'clock in the morning and me and two other chaps went into this store and stole some cigarettes. That was about all we stole. I had never done anything wrong before and I've never done anything like it since. The only problem was I was with a known criminal, a well-known lad. I actually got sentenced with him. The third guy that was with us, he turned Queen's Evidence. He stood up in the dock and said we had done this and done that. What the police did was put about thirty or forty other cases on top of us that we didn't do, they just fitted us up for that and we didn't have a leg to stand on. They cleared their books and got rid of two rogues.

'So, one Saturday morning, I was refereeing a football match at the borstal when this chap came out and said, "Get in and get changed, you've got a visitor." I said I wasn't expecting anyone, because you usually had to send out passes to get a visitor. He says, "You have a visitor and that's it." Most of these visits were taken in the common room, but the PO (Prison Officer) came along and said, "Your visitor is in my office." I didn't know what the heck was going on. Anyway I went in and P J is there. He introduced himself to me, gave me ten cigarettes, sat down, spoke to me for ten minutes, got up and left and that was it.'

Gerard was completely disoriented. Paddy swept in like a whirlwind, with a flurry of weightless, insignificant words that floated around Gerard's head, and then, seemingly within minutes, he was gone.

'I was totally bewildered. We were only together for ten minutes. We didn't shake hands, we didn't do anything. We just talked about something, I don't even remember what, and that was it, away he went. He came that once and then he disappeared and I never saw him again for nearly forty years.'

Paddy could not recall ever having met Gerard until days before they were reunited, forty years later in 2002. News of Gerard's re-emergence stirred Paddy's memory. Dimly at first, faint memories came to Paddy of the meeting in the borstal. Then the thoughts came flooding back from the dark recesses of his mind, where they had been securely imprisoned, untouched, for four decades. Out of self-preservation, Paddy had shut out and closed off access to those painful memories he could not process.

'It was Harold Rankin, he told me about Gerard,' he remembers. 'Harold was told by one of the wardens down at the borstal. Harold called me into his office one day and said, "Paddy, you have a brother and he wants to see you. He's down in the borstal." And I says, "I'm not going anywhere near a borstal, I don't know anybody. As far as I'm concerned I have nobody." Harold told me to go down to the borstal anyway; he said, "Sure, it'll do you no harm."'

Paddy had complete trust in Harold and, if he assured him that this guy was his brother and that he should see him, then he would go.

'So I hopped on the bus. I remember getting that Ulsterbus, I remember it very well now. I can even tell you what I wore that day — I wore a grey suit. I remember going through the big gates and into the wee room — there were two or three people in it. I remember him having really black hair, our Gerard; he had no moustache in those days.'

Paddy was on autopilot. He couldn't quite believe that he was actually sitting face to face with his brother.

'I had mixed reactions. I asked myself, is this really happening, is this true? As soon as I went in, I said to myself that I shouldn't be here. That's actually what I was saying to myself while I was talking away to him.'

Paddy didn't know what to do. He couldn't wait to get out of there. While he initially convinced himself that it was the idea of being in a borstal that scared him, it was actually the shock of discovering that he had a sibling.

'So I came back again and I told Harold I was not going back there. But it wasn't actually meeting him, it was the borstal idea. It put me off. I had been through all these years with not knowing my mother and father. I believed there was nobody belonging to me.'

The brief encounter remained buried in the darkest depths of Paddy's mind until he received that letter forty years later. In September 1964, the year after Gerard and Paddy's first meeting, Gerard was given the option of early release from the borstal if he would move to England. He was serving a three-year sentence of which he had completed fourteen months, and the prospect of escaping the remaining year-and-a-half was too tempting to pass up. A new scheme had been introduced whereby young offenders were offered the chance of early parole and, as a model prisoner, Gerard was an ideal candidate.

'I did exactly fourteen months, eleven days and seven hours,' he says. 'I was the first young person in Northern Ireland to get out under this new scheme. It was 12 September. I should have by right done another seven or eight months before I was eligible for parole. I was allowed to take part in the scheme because I was actually leaving from the borstal to go to England. If I had been coming back into Newry, or any other part of Northern Ireland, I wouldn't have got on it. My sister came across from Liverpool and said that she had a job for me and asked if there was any chance that I could be released early. I was a model prisoner as well, so everything was going for me. So they let me out.'

Gerard was free to go but the borstal wardens wanted to ensure that he actually left the country and didn't abscond. They went to great lengths to safely deliver the young delinquent to his destination.

'I had a detective who came with me to the boat, got on the boat with me, and said cheerio to me at Liverpool docks. He actually came across with me to make sure I got off. I seriously wasn't that dangerous,' he roars with laughter.

Gerard left Ireland, intending never to return. He stayed in Liverpool for a few years and then moved to Birmingham where he met his wife, Bernadette. Over the course of the next few years the couple had three children: Stephanie, Gerard and Colm.

Gerard also ran a successful business involved in industrial maintenance in factories.

In 2000 he sold the business and retired to the small British Midlands village of Kingstone in Hereford, where he took on a small post office and off-licence. His intention to retire to the quiet life did not pan out exactly the way he planned.

'I sold up and retired when I was fifty-five, intended to take it easy. I've ended up in this post office and stores and I'm doing more hours than I've ever done in my life. That's ironic. What I'm doing down here is working seven days a week; it's bit of a bind as such. But it's a beautiful part of the world. I'm in a village and right next door to a pub.'

The discovery of his long-lost brother was as much a shock to him as it was to Paddy. In fact, Gerard knew nothing about the breakthrough in locating Paddy until his son, Gerard, told him about it. He had taken it upon himself to find his uncle. He had long listened to his dad's wish to trace his brother.

'I didn't even know Gerard was looking for Paddy. I always knew Paddy was around somewhere but, as time goes on, the less you think about it. I think he did it more for his own personal reasons. He wanted to satisfy his own curiosity about my background. I never really discussed my background or even gave it much thought. It never really bothered me. I think Gerard was just curious, more curious than me.'

Much like his half-brother Joe, whom he was yet to learn about, Gerard was enjoying life as a grandfather to his three grandchildren, Daniel, Joseph and Gerard, when his son tracked Paddy down.

'I didn't know anything about the search. The first time I

found out was when he told me he had found him. It was nice to know that he was about,' Gerard says simply. Learning about Joe on the other hand was a complete shock. 'I was surprised more than anything else, total surprise. I never knew he existed.'

Joe was similarly shocked. He had found it very difficult to take on board that Paddy was his half-brother and was just about coming to terms with that when another one came out of the woodwork.

'It was bad enough finding out I had a brother when I believed I was the only one in the family — then finding another one! I thought, how many more are hidden under the carpet?' he says. 'After sixty years, when you find out something like that, you just don't cotton on to it. I was saying to myself, "I don't believe it. Somebody is having me on here."'

11

WHEN THE INITIAL shock of learning about each other wore off, the three brothers decided to meet. Eddie and Gerard arranged for a get-together at the Ivanhoe Hotel in Carryduff, outside Belfast. It was a warm Friday evening as Eddie and his wife, Susan, settled into seats in the hotel's reception area to wait for Gerard and his wife, Bernadette. Paddy was being ferried down in the Polio Fellowship's bus and had not arrived yet. Gerard was a little late and Eddie was worried that he had gotten lost on his way up from Newry, and when he arrived, Eddie and Susan were relieved to see him. They ordered a drink and waited for Paddy. The air of anticipation was soon dispersed as the Fellowship's bus pulled up outside. Paddy, with a bunch of flowers in his lap for Bernadette, manoeuvred his wheelchair up the ramp and into the hotel foyer. Gerard and Bernadette rose to greet him. There were introductions, warm handshakes and smiles; the scene Paddy had been waiting for his entire life was unfolding before his eyes. The two brothers were at last reunited.

Eddie, who had witnessed Paddy's meeting with Joe, felt that when Gerard and Paddy met there was an instant connection.

'There was an immediate bond, much more so than with Joe, but then Gerard had met Paddy before when they were younger,' Eddie recalls. 'Gerard had been doing the looking and Paddy was quite happy to meet him whereas with Joe it was thrust on him.'

Eddie also felt confident that Gerard and Paddy were full brothers.

'They had similar mannerisms. Gerard's wife said later that night that, although they didn't look anything alike, when she was watching Paddy, his mannerisms were awfully like Gerard's.'

When Paddy and Gerard had met back in 1963, Paddy was a slim, five foot, four inches teenager with long black hair who carried himself with the cumbersome walk of the calliper-wearer. Gerard was skinny himself but a good four or five inches taller than Paddy. In the four decades that had passed, both brothers had changed considerably. Paddy's shoulder length locks were long gone, replaced with tightly-cropped white hair. Gerard's own ebony tresses had long since given way to a dark shade of grey but still had a wisp of life about them in the form of a stray curl which snaked across his forehead. A neat white moustache, not present when he and Paddy originally met, outlined his cheery smile and lit up his eyes and rosy cherub-like cheeks. Time had filled out both brothers and each now sported a generous midriff. Paddy's callipers had been traded for a wheelchair and his younger brother's warm presence towered over him. As the evening progressed the siblings gradually eased into each other's company. Paddy confesses that after a few hours with Gerard he felt closer to him than he had to Joe.

'We talked in general about old times. About the borstal, what he was doing, what I was doing. I felt closer to him because he was my full brother. I felt that a half-brother wasn't really the same. It was just different with Gerard,' he says.

Eddie, Susan and Bernadette were very conscious that the brothers had many years to catch up on but it seemed that having others around them eased their transition from strangers to family.

As the night drew in Eddie and Susan left for home and Paddy, Gerard and Bernadette, who were spending the night in the Ivanhoe, headed off to bed. Making his way to his own room, the enormity of what the day had brought hit Paddy.

'I finally met Gerard. That I could go out of this world and say that I had somebody was very important to me,' he remembers.

The following evening Joe arrived with his wife, Ann, and their daughter, Joanne, and for the first time the three brothers were together in the same room. Paddy's friend, William, had also come down from Ballyclare to join them for dinner. There was an initial tension after the introductions, with no one exactly sure what was required of them. But with the customary Northern Irish response to every stress, drinks were ordered and the ice was broken.

'Everyone was on edge at the start but then we got into the swing of it and we had a very good evening,' Gerard recalls. 'It was a quite surreal at times. It's hard to imagine

— you are sitting with somebody who is not a mirror image of you but you are from the same stock. It was just very surreal.'

Joe found the whole situation quite overwhelming but he was relieved at how easily he got on with his newly-discovered half-brother.

'Gerard was a very nice guy, very down to earth. P J is very down to earth, too.'

Joe tried to find some likeness between himself and his half-brother but was at a loss to find one.

'I looked at Gerry and I didn't see any resemblance. I looked for something but there was nothing there to me.'

Ironically, while Paddy felt closer to Gerard, Gerard had the opposite feeling.

'I felt closer to Joe. I don't know why. I can't explain it. I can't quite put my finger on it. Paddy can be quite overpowering at times when he gets into full flow. Joe was easier going,' he says.

Joe's light-heartedness could have been explained by the fact that he did not want or expect anything from his newly-unearthed family. He was really only there out of a sense of curiosity and because he knew how much it meant to Paddy. Paddy, on the other hand, had a lot invested in this meeting. With years to fill in and puzzles to unravel, it wasn't long before the inevitable question arose over why their mother had left her three sons. As expected, no one had a satisfactory answer.

'Nobody seemed to know why she left us. Paddy was more interested in my mother than anybody else. Personally I didn't care, neither did Joe. Paddy wanted us to get involved, we didn't want to know.'

Paddy sensed his brothers' reluctance and disinterest.

The tone of the conversation and the emotion of the day took its toll on him and he retreated to the patio of the hotel. He had been waiting all his life for this moment and here it was.

Contrary to Joe's initial analysis one year before of how easily Paddy seemed to 'slip into' having a new family, Paddy found it very difficult to handle the fact that he really had a family to call his own. And here they were, laughing and joking together as if it was the most natural thing in the world. But it was his brothers' attitudes towards their mother's whereabouts which really upset and confused him. All he had ever wanted was to find her or her grave and make his peace but they had no interest in what had happened to her in the years since she'd walked out on them.

'I broke down and started to cry when they started talking about my mother,' he recalls. 'Gerard was saying that it didn't really bother him much. I had always wanted to find my mother's grave before I passed from this earth. He took a different view. He said he wouldn't be annoyed with it at all. Joe said that if we found any more relatives he didn't want to know. That really got to me, so I had to get out of the way for a while.'

Joe could tell Paddy felt the strain.

'He had no one and I knew he felt it. You could see the tears in his eyes when he could see the three of us together. He had to take his wheelchair out to the patio. Gerard got up first and followed him out. He broke down a bit.'

It was unsettling for these grown men to see another man, their brother, but ultimately a stranger, so upset and emotional, especially on what should have been such a joyous occasion.

'I asked him why and he says, "Seeing you all together,"'

Joe recalls. 'He didn't think he had anybody. He hasn't had anyone other than the people who cared for him.'

Joe and Gerard comforted Paddy as best they could and then left him so that he could rejoin them when he was ready. Gathering himself together Paddy took a deep breath, dried his eyes and moved back into the lounge. As he wheeled in he could hear gales of laughter from the corner where his brothers, their wives, and his friends were gathered. Never in his life could he have dreamed that he would be witnessing this.

It had been a very pleasant weekend with plenty of pictures taken to record the day when the three brothers had finally met. For Joe, it was an extraordinary experience and he was looking forward to life returning to normal. The past had been righted, at least a little, for Paddy and Gerard. While, to Paddy, a new family was gathering around him, to Gerard, there was a sense of closure.

'We had a nice weekend. It was a pleasant enough experience. I didn't get the feeling we were going to be bosom buddies or living in each other's pockets. It was closure. I thought okay, I've laid that one to rest. I was quite happy to carry on with my life. Joe was possibly thinking the same as I was. We met and that was it — leave well enough alone. But it was opening things up for Paddy and it was closing things for us. We had a different reaction to it. Paddy was pushing things towards finding our mother but Joe wasn't. I found that a little bit difficult. But we left on very, very good terms.'

Paddy recalls Joe jokingly remarking to him before he left, 'Don't you be finding anyone else.'

'But he meant it,' Paddy says with a hint of sadness.

For Joe and Gerard, who had grown up within a family and now had families of their own, their lives were drawing into their autumn days, but for Paddy, who had just found his family, he felt as if he was emerging into the spring of his life. New relationships were bursting through and he wanted to nurture them. In his heart he wished Philomena could have been there to see her three grown sons together.

'If my mother had been there, it would have made it perfect. Not so much my father, but my mother was the main one as far as I was concerned,' Paddy says. 'I'm all mixed up to this day about what happened to the two of them and why I was put in a home. It's a bit of a wrench for me. I don't think we'll ever know what happened, why she left us.'

12

PADDY'S SEARCH FOR his mother has turned his life upside down. In the past number of years he has had a nervous breakdown and numerous counselling sessions to relieve the anxiety that trying to find her has caused. Questions about her and her whereabouts have plagued his thoughts daily. Over the last few years he has been on a rollercoaster of emotions in his desperate search for Philomena and the unexpected discovery of his brothers. After being reunited with Joe and Gerard, no traces of his mother were found and the likelihood of meeting her face to face was diminishing. As that search drew to a close, Paddy had to accept that he had done all he could to answer his questions about her. It has been as much a quest to throw light on his own identity as locating his mother. By never really knowing himself, he was often unable to share the experiences that friends with families took for granted — discussing how their parents met, remembering summer holidays away with their family, looking at old pictures of their grandparents, reliving childhood adventures with cousins — endless scenarios he would never play a part in. Paddy has always been detached from this 'normality'.

Paddy opened the door to his self-contained flat, greeting Eddie and I with a big smile and a wheezy 'Hello.' He ushered us in and quickly zipped behind us with something akin to elegance in the electric wheelchair he has become so accustomed to. His movements are more fluid than my own or that of Eddie, who visibly carries the burdens of polio. His compact, ground floor flat is crammed with clocks. I counted six on my first visit but each time I return there seem to be more, all of varying sizes, colour and design, from the traditional carriage clock to a huge digital clock and radio.

'Why do you have so many clocks?' I asked him one day after numerous visits when formality had long since passed.

'I love clocks. I suppose it was because I never had a place of my own and when I finally did, I started collecting things and clocks were just one of those things,' he says, shrugging his shoulders, drawing a line under that question as if dispensed with.

Over the years, Paddy has become preoccupied with time, and the fact that for most of his life he has been living on somebody else's watch: fitting into other people's schedules and having no real control over his own life. Now, in his own home, after nearly sixty years, he has taken control over his life, and empowered himself to find the answers about his past that had eluded him for as long as he can remember.

It had been a long, lonely road before Paddy, at the age of

fifty-six, took his courage in hand and set in motion the events that led to Joe and Gerard. But the joy in finding his siblings was tinged with overwhelming feelings of sadness that Paddy was ill-equipped to deal with. The hope of building on the discovery of his brothers to find his mother was shattered when Joe and Gerard both expressed an explicit lack of interest in joining the search. With this, Paddy's world came crumbling down around him.

'The first time I had a nervous breakdown was a few years ago. The most recent one was around summer 2005,' Paddy says. 'Everything was building up on me. I was thinking too much about my mother. I had always been thinking about her, right through all of my days. It stuck in my mind.'

While not oblivious to the possibility that his mother, who would have been in her mid-eighties, could be dead, Paddy's overriding desire became to at least visit her grave to make his peace with her.

'Before I die, if I could just see my mother's grave, I would be a happy man. Our Gerard and Joe are different but I would definitely be a happy man. I would just spend about two hours there, talking to her, just having a quiet conversation, telling her that I forgive her. I would say that it's not her fault or anybody's fault. Some people put the blame on her; you have to be very careful.' A visibly emotional Paddy struggles to hold back the tears. 'I know now that it'll never happen, but you never know. That would be closure for me. It really would be.'

The frustration at not being able to find answers is a torture to Paddy. His brothers' indifference frustrates him further, making him feel all the more helpless. Their apparent apathy drives him to near despair.

'Gerard has no interest. If he found the graveyard tomorrow, where she's buried, he wouldn't go near it. I have no ill-will towards my mother. I would love to stand over her grave and say, "It's all in the past." She could still be alive,' he says, hopefully. 'She would be about eighty-five.

'I just want to know who she was. It would fill the void in my life. Gerard has no interest. He was adopted and got on well. I was a different kettle of fish. I was brought up through the system and what annoys me so much is that no one told me anything. To this very day I know nothing. I'd like to know what she looked like. Why I was put into care? What happened and why? Obviously, I was a wee abandoned. It's not my fault. I don't want to fill her with guilt. I have always made it clear that I just want to know what happened.

'If I ever meet her before I leave this world it would give me the greatest joy. I would embrace her and I would talk to her and see her part of the story. I would understand because I am very broad-minded,' he says, as if trying to convince himself, hoping maybe that his mother, wherever she is, might hear his words.

'Having lived all these years with that void in my life, going through all those homes and what I had to put up with, the biggest problem was love. I never had any. I can be very nasty and hard but I am a very kind person. I appreciate what people do for me. I get uptight and I worry about things.'

A year of counselling has opened Paddy's eyes to how his upbringing has reinforced his lack of self worth, and how his insecurities are a natural product of the environments he lived in. He has had to re-evaluate his life and offer some compassion to his younger self, whose only tool for survival was to harden his heart.

Being reunited with his brothers finally enabled him to let go of a little of that hard-heartedness and open himself up. He was no longer alone now that he had somebody he could call family.

'The difference it made meeting Gerard was amazing. Whenever I went into hospital, one of the questions on the form was "Who is your next of kin?" and I would have to say "nobody". The difference it made being able to say "Gerard"...,' he trails off, shaking his head at the wonder of it. 'You have no idea how it feels to say "I don't have anyone." All of a sudden I was able to say, "Well, I have a brother and his address is such and such." It makes a big difference when you actually have somebody. I can leave this world content, knowing that I have a family.'

For Gerard things have returned, more or less, to how they were before Paddy and Joe entered his life. He sympathises with Joe, for whom the whole 'long-lost brother' experience has been a complete shock. Indeed, the two have not spoken to each other since the day they met.

'He doesn't keep in touch and I don't keep in touch. It's sort of mutual on both sides,' Gerard says. 'He's not really enamoured with all this instant family and long-lost brother sort of thing. If you can sort of look at it in brackets, he was brought up in a kind of "normal situation" whereas I had an idea that there was somebody around along the way, having already met Paddy when we were younger.'

As for Paddy, Gerard knows that life has been hard for him but he is very aware that he needs something from him which he cannot give to help compensate for sixty years without a family. He understands this hunger but has nothing other than friendship to offer Paddy.

'I think he has locked a lot of the hurt and pain away from himself. I think that's how he copes with it. I told him, "You're a well balanced person; both chips on your shoulders are the same size,"' he laughs. Gerard notes that this 'wicked sense of humour' which he and his brother share has steered them through many of life's hardships.

'Well, let's be honest. Northern Ireland people have a very wicked sense of humour. You have to look at adversity and then get on with it. Paddy is a little bit possessive in different things and I think he feels, probably quite rightly, that's he's entitled to various things because of his history and his disability. But that's him and I wouldn't even think of trying to change him.'

Gerard has never been overly curious about his mother because to him she never really existed. He realises that because Paddy grew up without a mother, he feels compelled to get answers, but he doesn't have the same yearning.

'I don't particularly. He has. He said if only he could find her grave or something, something that he could mourn, or offload. But I haven't got that problem, you see, because I have never really given her any more than twenty seconds' thought in my life. As far as I was concerned, she didn't really exist.'

Gerard did wonder about her in his younger years but, growing up within a secure adoptive family, these thoughts gradually faded away and he was never really preoccupied with her disappearance.

'I may have thought about it when I was a young man but

I never dwelled on it in any fashion. It never bothered me. My attitude was that there must have been circumstances at the time. She must have had a reason. End of story.'

Joe has a similar outlook. For him life is gradually regaining a sense of normality after the upheaval of meeting his two brothers. He has had the odd telephone conversation with Paddy but no further contact with Gerard.

'Everything seems to be back to normal now. I still know they are there and I haven't forgotten about them. I send them cards at Christmas. I'm not one for keeping in contact with people. They're nice fellows, it's just unfortunate the way things are.'

Joe has always viewed Paddy's search for their mother as a bit of a lost cause. Just like Paddy, he grew up without his mother, but he had caring grandparents and a father to look after him, so her absence never loomed too largely in his life.

'I think P J is clutching at straws. How many people my age have mothers alive? I'm coming up on sixty-five, so she'd be nearly eighty-five. She was nothing to me. But with P J, it's a different kettle of fish. It's hard to take but you have to get on with your life. He has opened a book and I don't think he can close it. It's just unfortunate the way things happened. I was looked after and he wasn't. Gerard has done well for himself. He has settled down with a family and I have settled down with mine but P J still has no one.'

Joe has tried not to dwell too much on his mother's disappearance but her failure to contact him when he was a child has played on his mind. In particular, he wonders what went wrong between his mother and his father, Thomas.

'I would wonder why she never tried to contact me. She

did love my father at one time. I don't know what happened.'

A small part of Joe hoped Paddy's search would come up with some answers but he was not going to waste the precious time he had with his family to resurrect old ghosts.

'I think it is a near impossibility to find a grave. P J is trying to get an end to his story in life. I'd love it to be a good ending because I'd love to know myself what happened to her. But I've never pushed it. For P J it will always be in the back of his mind.'

Warnings that Paddy's search might prove fruitless in the end have come from all directions, including his close friends. William Auld believes Paddy left it too late to start digging up the past and has noticed how, over the last number of years, the more obsessed he became with his search, the more he fell victim to depression.

'I feel it was a bad idea to go down that route. Maybe when he was younger it might not have been a bad idea. But after sixty years, to find that there is a brother who lives ten miles away... He says he is suffering from depression now, so that could be the link. In hindsight, it mightn't have been the best idea. Over the last couple of years he has started looking at the dark side of things. I know a lot of things can happen to you. His education has suffered and his first instinct is to put the mitts up. But that's not his fault and he knows that.'

Paddy's one constant has been his friend, Eddie McCrory. Eddie has stayed by Paddy's side through all the ups and downs. He even understands Gerard and Joe's indifference to their mother.

'Paddy's original expectation was, if I just go to her grave and tell her I don't bear any grudges, then I'd be quite happy. I said to him that she might still be alive. I don't know if maybe I gave him the hope that she might be. But the difference between Paddy and the brothers was that Gerard had adoptive parents and Joe had his grandparents. Paddy had nobody and he needed somebody to have some sort of attachment to, no matter if it be a dead mother or whatever. I could see the difference between Paddy and his brothers. Paddy had the understanding initially that his parents' marriage was a mixed one and then he caught polio, so they couldn't cope, which was why he was put into care. He knows now that is unlikely. I think it has helped immensely, especially finding Gerard. He has somebody he can record as his next of kin.'

Just when it seemed that all was lost, and Paddy's search was destined to end in failure, a last ditch attempt to track down Philomena turned up an interesting lead. A letter appealing for information about her immediate family was printed in the *Irish News*, one of Belfast's daily newspapers. Initially, the appeal appeared fruitless. Then, one afternoon a couple of weeks later, a surprise phone call from Sydney, Australia, threw some new light on Paddy's mother. The man on the other end of line had been sent the newspaper clipping by his family in Belfast who, confused and shocked by its content, forwarded it to him. After a brief conversation he was able to confirm that he was Philomena's nephew and that Gerard was most likely named after his uncle Gerry.

Other than a vague notion that Philomena had moved to England in the 1950s he had no idea what had happened to her and whether she was still living. He voiced his family's concerns at Paddy's search, but said he'd explain that Paddy's only intention was to find his mother.

Unfortunately, as hopeful as the conversation was, a second correspondence from Australia stated that the family would prefer not to get involved in Paddy's search. His hopes were crushed once more. Paddy, despite understanding the family's reluctance to get involved, wished that they could still offer him something more.

Nevertheless, the search continued and many possible links emerged with the help of Belfast-based organisation, Adopt, which assists adoptees in tracing their birth parents. Unfortunately, none of these links led to Philomena Grimshaw. Then, Adopt researcher, Kathleen McClure, suggested sending a short e-mail with all the known facts about Philomena to a tracing agency in England which might be of some help in confirming whether she was alive or dead.

Twenty-four hours later, a brief reply confirmed that Philomena Grimshaw's death had been registered in Manchester in the March quarter of 1972. Her death certificate confirmed that she had been born Philomena Murray on 5 October 1922, was the wife of Thomas Grimshaw, and had lived at a Manchester address. Sadly, it was only in learning of his mother's death that Paddy would gain any glimpse into her life.

She had died on 31 January 1972 from mitral stenosis, a heart condition which, although quite rare now, occurs mostly in older people who had rheumatic fever as children and did not have access to antibiotics.

Philomena was only fifty years of age when she died, just one day after the horrific events of Bloody Sunday. It is not known whether she was alone when she died or whether she was in the company of friends from her adopted city. The irony was that, one year before her death, Paddy, sickened by the Troubles, and in a bid to strike it big on the music scene, had ventured over to Manchester to make a new life for himself. Unknown to him, his mother had been living in that very city at the very time of his visit. Paddy finds it hard to accept that he was so close to her yet had no idea they were walking the same streets.

'It's so strange, such a coincidence. If I had the slightest notion that she was there, then maybe I could have saved myself a lot of years of heartache and searching. I was at one end of the city and she was at the other. It's just hard to believe.'

Despite this cruel twist of fate, Paddy is glad to know at last where his mother's final resting place is.

'Wanting to find my mother was the closing chapter. It would be a closure to have found her. At least I know where she is. I'll never wonder for the rest of my days. That eases my mind. Maybe at some future date I'll go over to Manchester and look for her grave. I don't know; when you're disabled it's a hard job to get about and get things done. At least I'm satisfied in my mind that she is resting in peace.'

Despite finding her grave, what Paddy can't chase from his mind is the torrent of questions about why his mother left him in the first place. His relief at finally having located her is tainted by the reality that his one hope for answers is gone. He feels cheated.

'I still want to find out why I was put into the home. That's my biggest worry. But I'll never know that. I had hopes I was going to find her but I have no animosity. Things are the way they are. It's just part of life. But when I was younger it wasn't part of life to me. I was always wondering and wondering, trying to figure out what the problem was with me. That was because I was in all these stupid homes. But then, at the end of the day, at least I had somewhere. I could have been out on the streets. That's the way you look at it.'

He still feels cheated out of a normal life, but, at last, he is beginning to piece together a past, which is going some way to freeing his mind for the future.

'If I can't find out what I need to know, life will just have to go on. I'm just disappointed that my half-brother and full brother have no interest in our mother. What upset me was that they made more of their lives than I did, professionally and family-wise. But what doing this book has done for me is unbelievable. It has sort of made a picture for me now. It has definitely helped me in that respect. Bless God when it is all finished, I'll be okay and I'll know how things were. I'll have some answers. If I can't find out why my mother put me into care I'll just have to deal with it. I'm not going to make a big issue out of it.'

Paddy's compulsion to find answers is quite normal, according to Eilish Manning of Adopt, but she warns that what he thinks he wants to know may not bring him peace.

'It takes quite a while for information like "your mother is dead" to sink in. Rather than that bringing closure, it actually often exacerbates things. And the questions build: why, why, why, why? He thinks he wants to know all about why he was put into care. No doubt he does want to know that, but even if he does get that information it may not bring him the often used word, closure.'

Paddy's frustrations with his brothers' unwillingness to seek answers about their mother's life are also understandable.

'Often with new-found siblings you find that they have

no great interest in starting up a new relationship with their adopted brother or sister other than they are delighted to have met them. This is very hard on the sibling who has been adopted or in care,' Eilish says.

'There are people who will make demands on their new family, demands that the birth family are neither capable nor willing to meet. Often the birth family has been living unaware of this adopted sibling and it is very difficult for them to welcome this sibling into their family without any upset.

'At the end of the day you can't be unadopted, so the person placed in care or adopted has to get their head around the fact that they can't force their will for change on their birth family. But it is very difficult. Nobody knows what it's like to be adopted unless they have walked in their steps.'

For Paddy, his battle with the restrictions of his disability has compounded his feelings of being short-changed in life.

'The main problem with me was that, if I had been able-bodied, it would have been a different ball game altogether. But with me being disabled and being put into care, the two things combined didn't help. I never was a complainer. With this all being out in the open now it enlightens me.'

Paddy intends to visit his mother's grave one day, but when he does, he will do it alone — without his brothers. Hopefully then, he might find some of the answers he has spent his life searching for.

'I will go and see her grave. It'll be the final closure. I won't be getting the rest of the family involved. I'll just do it myself and make my peace.'

It may never be known what became of Philomena

Grimshaw after she left her husband and two-year-old son, Joe, abandoned her second son, Paddy, and gave her third son up for adoption. Joe's suspicions point to Philomena having had an affair, of which Paddy is believed to have been the product. Joe's grandparents insinuated that Philomena was a 'night-time girl' who loved going to dances and socialising while her husband was on shift work. These suspicions are compounded by the fact that, on 4 September 1944, a number of months after her separation from her husband, she gave birth to Paddy. There are any number of scenarios to suggest who Philomena might have had an affair with, if this was indeed the case.

Thomas Grimshaw is listed as Paddy's father on his birth certificate. However, the address at which Paddy's mother is supposed to have lived (Wilton Street, off the Shankill Road) was registered to a man — not Thomas — until 1967.

With the presence of American soldiers in the north during the war-torn 1940s, it is also possible that the fun-loving twenty-year-old, already dismayed at what family life had to offer, could have been seduced by the charms of a 'G I Joe'. But why Philomena put Thomas's name on Paddy's birth certificate if he was not the father leaves some room for doubt. The shame of having another man's child while married to Thomas is one explanation; another is that Paddy *was* Thomas Grimshaw's son. That she gave birth to a third son the year following Paddy's birth, when she had been separated from Thomas for over a year, muddies the waters still further. The reasons why this young mother left her sons behind have gone with her to the grave.

While Paddy may feel disappointment at never having actually met his mother, his friends believe that it is she who should have felt sadness for never having actually met him.

William Auld admires Paddy for facing up to his challenges in life and overcoming them.

'He has had a difficult life. A lot of outside circumstances have affected him. I think he has done very well. In Ballyclare everybody knows him. He's a good communicator. Everybody likes him. You couldn't wish for anything more.'

Paddy's old landlady, Jenny Bradford, agrees that he has a special way of endearing people to him.

'Pat has had an interesting life. On the main street in Ballyclare, he sees everybody and everybody knows him. Everybody has a yarn with him.'

Paddy is left with is an image of Philomena Grimshaw as a short plump woman with black hair and a pretty face. Maybe, one day, if he's over at Old Trafford to see his team, Manchester United, play, he might just take a taxi to the cemetery where his mother lies, waiting to meet her son.

Recent Titles
from
The Brehon Press

IN WAR AND PEACE

The Story of Corrymeela

ALF McCREARY

foreword by Ray Davey

"My spirit is with you and please carry on your work tirelessly. You can consider me a member of your Community."

—The Dalai Lama

Throughout the years of the Troubles, Corrymeela gained acknowledgement worldwide for its efforts in promoting peace against a background of ongoing turmoil. Now, with the guns silenced and the politicians talking together, the Centre on the North Antrim coast faces new challenges. In this frank and timely book, acclaimed journalist Alf McCreary traces the forty-year history of Corrymeela, telling of its often fraught efforts to spread the "pollen of peace".

"Corrymeela set an agenda and was uncompromising in what that agenda was. It was an utter belief in the capacity of the human person to change for the better."

—President Mary McAleese

"Alf McCreary is ideally placed to take an independent view of Corrymeela over the past forty years. What a story he has to tell!"

—Reverend Ray Davey, Founder of Corrymeela

ISBN 978 1 905474 15 8, £8.99 paperback

TWICE ROUND ON THE HOBBY HORSE

A Memoir

ANITA ROBINSON

"I WAS A 'WEE LATE ONE'. BORN FOURTEEN-AND-A-HALF YEARS AFTER THE REST OF THE FAMILY, I CAUSED A MINOR SENSATION. IN FACT MY MOTHER THOUGHT I WAS THE MENOPAUSE ... "

Anita Robinson's story, which charts her journey from a rural upbringing, through a career as a teacher in the Creggan and Carnhill parishes in Derry, to becoming a renowned local writer and broadcaster, is both a classic account of childhood and a witty take on the world in which the post-war "baby boomers" now find themselves.

Vivid and hilarious sketches of growing up, getting married and having children are combined with wry observations on child-rearing, relationships, teaching, and everyday life in the modern age.

Funny and unforgettable, *Twice Round on the Hobby Horse* breathes new life into the Irish memoir.

ISBN 978 1 905474 13, £8.99 paperback

YESTERDAY'S GLOVEMEN

The Golden Days of Ulster Boxing

BRIAN MADDEN

Ulster has had its fair share of sporting champions over the years, and nowhere is this more evident than in the squared circle. Names such as Rinty Monaghan, Jim "Spider" Kelly, Bunty Doran, Ike Weir and Johnny Caldwell still evoke fond memories of classic fights from the golden age of local boxing. In this entertaining book, Brian Madden charts the careers of twenty-five "glovemen", from world champions to journeymen pugilists, in a personal selection of both the cream of the crop and the stalwarts of the supporting bill. Illustrated throughout with many of the fights and fighters of yesteryear, the result is a must-read for any boxing enthusiast.

Boxers featured are:
Mickey Lavery, Jack Garland, Jim "Spider" Kelly, Pat Maurice Marrinan, Ike Weir, Rinty Monaghan, Bunty Doran, Al Gibson, Paddy Slavin, Tom Meli, Bob Gourley, Bunty Adamson, Paddy Graham, Sammy Cowan, Charlie Cosgrove, David Irving, Francis "Fra" McCullagh, Henry Turkington, Jim McCann, Johnny Caldwell, Jimmy Carson Snr, Jimmy Carson Jnr, Billy "Spider" Kelly, John Kelly.

ISBN 1 905474 02 4, £16.99 hardback

THE BLOODY NORTH

Infamous Ulster Murder Cases

SEAN M[c]MAHON

Despite the association with political violence that has characterised its recent past, Ulster has also a strong history of "ordinary murder". Whether committed as a consequence of greed, lust, jealousy or pride, the last few centuries in the northern province are littered with bloody incidents of shooting, stabbing and battering.

In this compelling book, fourteen stories of murder most foul - including cases as diverse as the stalking and slaughtering of Mary Anne Knox by her possessive "lover", the killing of the widely unpopular Third Earl of Leitrim, the brutal tale of Robert the Painter, and the controversial slaying of Patricia Curran - are told, showing how real life (and death) can often be as fascinating as anything to be found in the pages of an Agatha Christie mystery.

Ripped from the headlines of the day and based on actual contemporary accounts, *The Bloody North* provides compulsive and thrilling reading for any true crime fanatic.

ISBN 978 1 905474 14 0, £7.99 paperback

WRITTEN IN STONE
A History of Belfast City Cemetery

TOM HARTLEY

The history of Belfast City Cemetery in many ways reflects the history of the city of Belfast itself, charting as it does the major events and personalities, as well as the attitudes and social conditions that have prevailed over the years. Politicians and businessmen, inventors and industrialists, Orangemen and republicans, the privileged and the pauper - divided in life by ideology or creed, wealth or social standing - now share the same sacred spread of clay in graves that are notable either for their grandiose architecture or touching simplicity.

In this unique book, Tom Hartley, the creator of the Belfast City Cemetery tours, tells the stories behind the names that grace the tombs and gravestones in what is regarded as a Protestant cemetery in an overwhelmingly Catholic neighbourhood. Key events, such as the First and Second World Wars, the battle over Home Rule, the flu and cholera epidemics, and the Troubles, are examined alongside the personal stories of those individuals whose role in these events inevitably cost them their lives.

Illustrated throughout with many photographs, documents and maps, this is an important addition to our local history.

ISBN 978 1 905474 18 9, £9.99 paperback